ADVANCE PRAISE FOR

Re-mapping Literary Worlds

"Ingrid Johnston has created a compelling research text from her intensive collaborative classroom-based work with Meg, a high school English teacher. Weaving the field texts into a metaphorical journey, Johnston creates a text that takes readers from her early years in South Africa to a multicultural high school in Canada. As a reader of her book, I was shown the continuities and discontinuities as she moved skillfully within the dimensions of time and place, the personal and the social. The research is a work of the borderlands—borderlands we are coming to recognize both in curriculum theory and in educational research. For students of narrative inquiry and of curriculum theory, it is a must read."

Jean Clandinin, Professor and Director,
Centre for Research for Teacher Education and Development,
University of Alberta, Edmonton, Alberta, Canada

"In *Re-mapping Literary Worlds,* Ingrid Johnston invites her readers to join her on a journey of inquiry into the role and potential of postcolonial literature in the educational preparation of school youth. Johnston's journey ranges across a wide intellectual terrain connecting literature, pedagogy, and philosophy with the latest insights in postcolonial theory. *Re-mapping Literary Worlds* is an excellent book. Johnston writes with a marvelous succinctness and fluidity of style about the very complex matters of place, identity, experience, and the production and arrangement of school knowledge in the modern educational context marked as it is by radical imperatives of globalization, electronic mediation, migration, and cultural pluralism. *Re-mapping Literary Worlds* is an exemplary piece of interdisciplinary scholarship. Johnston is able to integrate theoretical, empirical, and practical perspectives with great facility and rigor. I highly recommend this book to academics and educational practitioners alike."

Cameron McCarthy, Research Professor and University Scholar,
Institute of Communications Research, University of Illinois

"*Re-mapping Literary Worlds* is an invaluable guide for English teachers who want to develop their knowledge and practice in teaching postcolonial literatures. Beginning with the premise that major reforms are needed in teacher education in order to move English syllabi away from a narrow traditional base, this book offers an accessible but conceptually sophisticated and historically well-grounded perspective on the place of postcolonial studies in the English classroom. It is a timely study that shows how the contemporary teaching of English must engage with a significant reconfiguration of books, theories, and pedagogic practice."

John Stephens, Acting Dean, College of Humanities and Social Sciences, Macquarie University, Sydney, New South Wales, Australia

Re-mapping Literary Worlds

Studies in the
Postmodern Theory of Education

Joe L. Kincheloe and Shirley R. Steinberg
General Editors

Vol. 213

PETER LANG
New York • Washington, D.C./Baltimore • Bern
Frankfurt am Main • Berlin • Brussels • Vienna • Oxford

ingrid johnston

Re-mapping Literary Worlds

postcolonial pedagogy in practice

PETER LANG
New York • Washington, D.C./Baltimore • Bern
Frankfurt am Main • Berlin • Brussels • Vienna • Oxford

Library of Congress Cataloging-in-Publication Data

Johnston, Ingrid.
Re-mapping literary worlds: postcolonial pedagogy in practice /
Ingrid Johnston.
p. cm. — (Counterpoints; v. 213)
Includes bibliographical references and index.
1. Literature—Study and teaching (Secondary)—Canada.
2. Canon (Literature) I. Title: Remapping literary worlds.
II. Title. III. Counterpoints (New York, N.Y.); v. 213.
PN71.C2 J64 807'.1'271—dc21 2002022495
ISBN 0-8204-5752-3
ISSN 1058-1634

Die Deutsche Bibliothek-CIP-Einheitsaufnahme

Johnston, Ingrid:
Re-mapping literary worlds: postcolonial pedagogy in practice /
Ingrid Johnston.
–New York; Washington, D.C./Baltimore; Bern;
Frankfurt am Main; Berlin; Brussels; Vienna; Oxford: Lang.
(Counterpoints; Vol. 213)
ISBN 0-8204-5752-3

Cover design by Lisa Barfield

The paper in this book meets the guidelines for permanence and durability
of the Committee on Production Guidelines for Book Longevity
of the Council of Library Resources.

© 2003 Peter Lang Publishing, Inc., New York
275 Seventh Avenue, 28th Floor, New York, NY 10001
www.peterlangusa.com

Printed in the United States of America

To my daughters
Tonya and Bronwen

Table of Contents

Acknowledgments ix

Introduction: Overview of a Journey: Mapping the Territory 1

Mile One: Charting a Course: Under African Skies 7

Mile Two: Surveying the Scene: International Contexts
for Multicultural Literary Education 13

Mile Three: Sites of Representation: Culture, Race,
Gender, and Ethnicity 27

Mile Four: The Last "Post"? Postcolonialism and Literary Education .. 35

Mile Five: Territories of Desire: Contesting Canons 41

Mile Six: Literary Theory at the Crossroads 49

Mile Seven: Travelers' Tales: Teachers Testing Theories 61

Mile Eight: Traveling Companions: Research Revelations 73

Mile Nine: Voices En Route: Students and Texts in Dialogue 83

Mile Ten: A Sense of Place: Photo/graphs of a Grade 10 Class 97

Mile Eleven: Crossing Fictional Borderlands: *Obasan* and the
Construction of Personal Identity 115

Mile Twelve: Localities of the Everyday: Pedagogical Perspectives... 125

Mile Thirteen: Revisioning the Journey of Postcolonial Pedagogy 135

Appendices 149

References 155

Index 167

Acknowledgments

This book was made possible by the dedication and generosity of "Meg," the English teacher who traveled much of this pedagogical journey with me. To Meg, and to her high school students who participated in the research, I offer my sincere thanks.

Many colleagues, friends, and graduate students played a significant role in enabling this book to be written. Particular thanks go to Margaret Mackey, Anna Altmann, John Oster, Jill McClay, and Rebecca Luce-Kapler for their wonderful insights and unfailing generosity in listening and commenting on drafts of the writing. I also appreciate the support offered at various stages of this work by Stephen Arnold, Jean Clandinin, Terry Carson, Marg Iveson, George Richardson, Dennis Sumara, Tom Kieren, Elaine Simmt, Patrick Dias, Jyoti Mangat and Stephen Slemon.

I would like to offer special words of gratitude to Mary-Lee Judah who worked for many months formatting the text. Her unfailing patience and helpful advice were far more than I deserved. This book would not have been completed without her able assistance.

My family has offered constant love and support for my scholarly endeavors. My parents, Judy and Eddy, offered encouragement from afar, and my husband, Les, provided generous help with all aspects of the book. I am very grateful to my sister-in-law, Deidré, for transcribing my research tapes so carefully. My appreciation also goes to my daughters, Tonya and Bronwen, for their loving interest, and to their husbands, Robb and Jon, who helped to keep my computer running. Special thanks go to Robb for providing artistic ideas for the book cover. My little grandsons, Damon and Sebastien, provided fun and distraction when the writing became tedious or overwhelming.

A final note of gratitude for the financial assistance provided by the Social Sciences and Humanities Research Council of Canada and by the Izaak Walton Killam Memorial Scholarship.

Introduction

Overview of a Journey: Mapping the Territory

[T]he application of the metaphor of travel to thought conjures up the image of an innovative mind that explores new ways of looking at things or which opens up new horizons. That mind is a critical one to the extent that its moving beyond a given set of preconceptions or values also undermines those assumptions. Indeed, to call an existing order (whether epistemological, aesthetic, or political) into question by placing oneself "outside" that order, by taking a "critical distance" from it, is implicitly to invoke the metaphor of thought as travel.

Georges Van den Abbeele (1992, xiii)

A map, then, is only a life of conversations about a forgotten list of irretrievable selves.

Dionne Brand (2001, 224)

For much of the twentieth century, canonized texts from Britain and, more recently, from the United States inscribed the Canadian high school literary map. During the past decades, Canadian students have had increasing access to a national literature, but for many immigrants to Canada from non-Western countries, first-generation Canadians, Native Canadians, and other minority students, gaps and absences remain in the literary landscape. There are few opportunities for these students to connect with texts that may resonate with their own cross-cultural histories and traditions and even fewer opportunities for them to engage critically in deconstructing texts that misrepresent or exoticize the experiences of non-Western people.

This book is a literary journey that steps briefly into the past, pauses to consider the present, and attempts to envision the future of postcolonial literary studies in Canadian secondary schools. The focus of my journey is an exploration of possibilities for enlarging the traditional Western canon of literature taught in Canadian high schools and of the consequences of using postcolonial reading strategies to encourage both minority and mainstream students to cross cultural boundaries. The study took place over a period of three school terms in the mid-1990s, working with two grade 12 classes, one grade 11 Advanced Placement class, and two grade 10 classes in a large Western Canadian inner-city school with a diverse student population.

At the heart of the research is a collaborative relationship between two English teachers: Meg, a practicing English teacher, and myself, a researcher. Together, we made text selections of international literature and decided on teaching strategies that might enable students to critically examine literary representations and ideologies. As a participant observer in Meg's classes during the teaching of the postcolonial texts, I listened to students' discussions of the literature and read their personal and critical written responses. In subsequent interviews with student volunteers from all five classes, I asked them to reflect on their responses to the selected texts and to consider links between the literature and their own lives.

Three primary questions are pondered throughout this research journey:

- What are the positive values for students from diverse cultures of engaging with literary texts that resonate with their own histories, traditions, and cross-cultural experiences? What are the concomitant drawbacks?
- How might reading and deconstructing postcolonial literature in the context of a classroom enable students and teachers to problematize representations of self, place, and the "other" in literary texts?
- What challenges and difficulties does one teacher face as she attempts to introduce postcolonial literature to students and to engage them in deconstructive reading strategies?

The metaphor of a journey, or a voyage, seems particularly apt as a description of this research. As Van den Abbeele (1992) suggests, the voyage is one of the most cherished institutions of Western civilization and culture.

> The dearest notions of the West nearly all appeal to the motif of the voyage: progress, the quest for knowledge, freedom as freedom to move, self-awareness as an Odyssean enterprise, salvation as a destination to be attained (typically straight and narrow). Yet if there is such a great cultural investment in the voyage, that locus of investment is nonetheless one whose possibility of appropriation also implies the threat of expropriation. The voyage endangers as much as it is supposed to assure these cultural values. (xv)

The very notion of travel presupposes a movement away from some place, a displacement, a rupture, a crossing of boundaries. A journey, like good research, has a powerful ability to dislodge the framework in which it is placed; it always takes us somewhere, but not necessarily where we planned to go.

Each milestone of my journey offers new vistas to explore. Some vistas will be literary, some political, some philosophical, some theoretical, some practical, and all speculative. In selecting these particular vistas, I do not attempt to create a linear, unified, or objective story that will offer a clearly defined path to new "truths" or knowledge. Rather, my journey will be a postmodern, reflexive narrative that seeks to carve out new conceptual routes, creating what C.T. Patrick Diamond (1995) calls a "bricolage" (81) of theories, remembrances, reflections, literary selections, descriptions of teaching practices, teacher and student voices from which readers can construct their own story of my research journey.

The power of story and a narrative mode of inquiry offer the potential to create such a research journey. Narrative and language are two of the main cultural processes shared by all societies. Both are ways of helping us to make sense of our experience. A story, Bruner (1990) reminds us, is always somebody's story; stories inevitably have a narrative voice and events are viewed through a particular set of personal prisms. To use the narrative mode is to "deal with the stuff of human action and human intentionality" and inevitably to consider "the vicissitudes, uncertainties and consequences of lived experiences" (37).

Stories and narrative link the worlds of thought and feeling. Whether personal or fictional, they attach us to others and to our own histories by providing what Witherell and Noddings (1991) describe as "a tapestry rich with threads of time, place, character…created through images, myths, and metaphors" (1). Stories offer us pictures of real people in real situations, struggling with real problems. They invite us to speculate on what might be changed and with what effect. Using the narrative mode, qualitative researchers work with teachers in a common quest to "rediscover the qualities, the complexities, and the richness of life in classrooms" (Eisner 1988, 20).

Narrative inquiry, as described by Connelly and Clandinin (1988), recognizes that teachers' lives are embedded within particular cultures and histories. It values "personal practical knowledge" in teacher research, taking into consideration an individual's prior knowledge and acknowledging the contextual nature of that teacher's knowledge (25). This kind of educational research requires the embodiment of theory in action. It acknowledges that teachers can transform the static knowledge of curriculum into pedagogically powerful knowledge capable of being adapted to variations in abilities and backgrounds of students. As Grumet (1988) suggests, curriculum can mediate between individual and world and thereby "span the chasm presently separating our public and private worlds" (xv).

Stories are crucial, both for making sense of others' lives, as in the research process, and for trying to make sense of our own lives. Diamond (1995) theorizes narrative as "one of the maps available for constructing a self through searching experience for meaning" (79). In a postmodern world, the new routes that are created in this search for meaning, which were once thought to lead to knowledge, are recognized as illusions. The map we follow, as Diamond claims, "merely suggests promising directions along which we might look and then stroll," and the narratives we create become a "never-ending construction of meaning" (81). History in this view is seen as inevitably ambiguous and reality is always an idiosyncratic patchwork. Narrative moves from being a linear representation of reality to an art form whose power lies in its contradictoriness. As Steiner (1995) suggests, "[Narrative] both is and is not a part of reality; it both is and is not a representation of reality; it both acts on and is irrelevant to politics and history" (118). Stories that we tell of our experiences are thus always fragmentary and incomplete, with conspicuous gaps, absences, and inconsistencies in the presented text. As Bruner (1990) writes, the status of stories "even when they are hawked as 'true' stories, remains forever in the domain midway between the real and the imaginary" (55).

In a poststructuralist narrative, such contradictions are acknowledged and a new form of text is privileged, one that moves beyond an ordered set of words within a book cover to become what Hayles (1989) calls "reservoirs of chaos" that invert traditional priorities so that "uncertainty is privileged above predictability and fragmentation is seen as the reality that arbitrary definitions of closure would deny" (314). My journey through this book, although of necessity linear in form, attempts to value this fluidity and indeterminacy. As I seek to re-search and re-represent the area of postcolonial theories and pedagogy, of classroom dynamics and teaching in a particular context, I accept that the boundaries between what is real and what is imaginary will always be shifting and elusive.

This research journey begins in South Africa in the 1970s where, as a white immigrant teacher from Britain, I first faced the dilemma of selecting literature for students living in a multicultural society and struggled with the effects of political and institutional constraints on the publication, availability, and teaching of indigenous and multicultural literary texts. My vista expands beyond the changing political and social scene in South

Africa to look at ways in which major Western countries have responded to new immigrant populations by introducing multicultural and antiracist education policies. Considerations of changing reading practices in Britain, the United States, and Canada within the framework of these new national policies lead into a recognition of the need to look beyond simplistic responses to diversity toward an understanding of how complex questions of representation are intertwined with issues of culture, race, gender, and ethnicity and with questions of subjectivity and identity.

Reflecting on the historical creation of "racial identities," I enter the debate over colonized people's search for an "ethnic essence" and an "authentic self" that contrasts with a more contemporary view of identity as necessarily ambivalent and hybrid. The claim that there is no "authentic" voice to be recovered from the colonized past leads me to consider the many tensions in postcolonial literary studies. In particular, my journey attempts to illuminate the tensions between a temporal dimension of postcolonialism that focuses on the changing literary scene in a postcolonial world and a theoretical dimension of postcolonial studies that links with poststructuralist critiques of essentialism and authenticity. Both these dimensions have important implications for canon reform and for new reading practices in Western countries.

My journey continues with an exploration of the literary canon debate, comparing contemporary critics who promote cultural pluralism with right-wing dissenters. I use the notion of a "nomadic" canon, which values the potential over the institutional, to consider how new ways of reading and deconstructing literary texts are challenging teachers to review both text selections and their theoretical perspectives on reading in the classroom.

I acknowledge on my journey the work of teachers and critics in Britain, the United States, and Canada who have already attempted to introduce a form of postcolonial pedagogy, and I consider the successes and limitations of such studies. These other studies lead into my own collaborative research with Meg and help to raise questions about the nature of the curriculum development in progress. What dilemmas does Meg encounter as she reinvents her curriculum? How much background knowledge does she need to teach postcolonial literature? Which teaching strategies seem to support canon expansion? How can she challenge her students to confront the (mis)representations of "others" in literary texts? Can she avoid stereotyping students from particular cultural backgrounds by expecting them to "represent" a culture in their responses to texts? Does reading and discussing antiracist literature raise students' political and social awareness of the inequities of the world and of their own positionings in the hierarchies of power? Is there a disjuncture between a "political" and an "aesthetic" response to literature? What of the future?

Meg's own discussions of her teaching, my journal entries and reflections, and students' written and oral responses to texts offer insights into a number of these questions and, inevitably, raise more questions for future studies on postcolonial pedagogy.

At mile thirteen, this particular research journey comes to an end, but as a narrative of postcolonial pedagogy, my research is only a small part of an ongoing narrative that attempts, as Freire (1970) suggests, to read words in order to read the world around us more critically and more compassionately. This journey has perhaps shaded in a small, floating segment on an ever-expanding global map whose flexible design, as explained by French poststructuralists Deleuze and Guattari (1987) may provide a useful metaphor for postcolonial discourse:

> The map is open and connectable in all its dimensions; it is detachable, reversi-
> ble, susceptible to constant modification. It can be torn, reversed, adapted to
> any kind of mounting, reworked by an individual, group, or social formation. It
> can be drawn on the wall, conceived of as a work of art, constructed as a politi-
> cal action or as a meditation. (12)

Drawing new maps, even within the confines of a classroom, enables us to understand how maps are productions of complex social forces that create and manipulate reality as much as they record it. Any such depiction or representation of an embodied sense, of a particular lived experience, includes a form of distortion. As Charles Taylor (1992) explains:

> The difference in question may be illustrated by the gap separating our inarticu-
> late familiarity with a certain environment (which enables us to make our way
> without hesitation) from the map that provides an explicit representation of this
> terrain. The practical ability exists only in its exercise, which unfolds in time
> and space....The map, on the other hand, lays out everything simultaneously,
> relating each and every point, one to another, without any discrimination what-
> soever....Maps or representations, by their very nature, abstract from lived time
> and space. (180)

In rejecting a reflectionalist model of cartography, which sees maps as passive reflections of the world, I choose rather to view them as "refracted images contributing to dialogue in a socially constructed world" (Harley 1988, 278). I hope my journey will contribute in a small way to an increased understanding of how a postcolonial literary education can enhance this dialogue.

Charting a Course:
Under African Skies

A map can tell me how to find a place I have not seen but have often imagined. When I get there, following the map faithfully, the place is not the place of my imagination. Maps, growing ever more real, are much less true.

Jeanette Winterson (1989, 81)

[Books] let me know firsthand that if the mind was to be the site of resistance, only the imagination could make it so. To imagine, then, was a way to begin the process of transforming reality. All that we cannot imagine will never come into being.

bell hooks (1991, 54–55)

As travelers in imaginative literary realms, readers cross the frontier of writing, the line that divides the everyday experiences of our lives from the imaginative representation of those experiences in fictional writing. Such transformations and understandings transcend the limited dimensions of charts and maps and offer readers of literature "a clarification, a fleeting glimpse of a potential order of things beyond confusion…a draught of the clear water of transformed understanding" (Heaney 1995, xv).

As a young and naïve high school English teacher in Durban, South Africa in the early 1970s, I tried to help my students cross that frontier by reading novels of Dickens and Hardy, plays of Shakespeare and Shaw, sonnets of Wordsworth and Donne, and short stories and poetry glorifying the hardships suffered by European settlers in the "primitive" Africa of the early twentieth century. My students were white, female, and pre-dominantly middle-class, a privileged minority group living in the midst of a politically unstable multiracial society with a rich diversity of cultures and traditions including Zulu, Sotho, and Xhosa. This narrow range of literature, written from a predominantly male European tradition, offered my students little of this cultural diversity. Their map of Africa was sterile, homogenous, dominated by a giant Union Jack that effectively blotted out the richness of the continent and served primarily to reinforce their ethnocentric view of the world and their own place in it.

A critical examination of books taught in South African senior schools during the apartheid era (Janks and Paton 1990) suggests that the literature selections were made largely according to the criterion of the Eurocentric notion of high culture, overlaid with strict Calvinist principles. Shakespeare, Dickens, Hardy, and Wordsworth formed the staple core of authors. There is little doubt that education departments in South Africa kept students away from the literature of their own country. As teachers, we were constrained to teach only those texts that were deemed "nonpolitical" and that presented a favorable portrait of the white government in South Africa. This policy divorced students from the realities of the society in which they lived. Janks and Paton explain:

> Much of the literature published in recent times by both black and white writers has been "political." Authors have portrayed again and again the hardships and injustices suffered by South Africans under the oppressive apartheid system. Three taboo subjects in South African schools are sex, politics and religion, and literature which deals too explicitly with these topics is considered suspect. The study of elitist British culture protects us from having to focus on the terrifying problems of the world in which we live. (1990, 241)

My reflections on my own teaching experiences in South Africa confirm Janks and Paton's views. More than twenty years after I left South Africa, I checked my bookshelves hoping to find some evidence of indigenous African texts among the books that I remembered reading at university and teaching in school. Hidden among my Chaucers, my Shakespeares, my Jane Austens, my Wordsworths, I found *The New Centenary Book of South African Verse* (Slater 1946). With increasing dismay, I read the preface and the poems that, no doubt, I offered my students as examples of African literature. The editor, after carefully explaining that he uses the term "South African poetry" to mean "poetry of South Africa, written in English" goes on to say,

> South Africa, being a new country, has not inherited that wealth of historical association, and romantic tradition which is the inevitable legacy of older civilisations. (vii)

Ignoring completely the rich legacy and oral traditions of any other cultures outside those of the "colonizers," the anthology is filled with nature poems of the beauty of the South African landscape and white men's struggles with the "natives." Could I really have suggested my students read poems such as Thomas Pringle's "The Kaffir"?

A Savage? Yes; though loth to aim at life,
Evil for evil he doth requite.
A Heathen? Teach him, then, thy better creed….(7)

What could my students have gained from reading this poem except a distorted view of Africa as an uncivilized country inhabited by a black race in need of "salvation"? There were, of course, innumerable examples of black African poets whose writing would admirably have denied every stereotype portrayed in *The New Centenary Book of South African Verse,* but these were unavailable and generally unknown in South Africa. Here, for example, in an excerpt from his poem "Amaguduka at Glencoe Station," Oswald Mbuyiseni Mtshali, who grew up close to my school in the province of Natal, conveys the sufferings of his people lyrically and ironically:

We are going to EGoli! EGoli! EGoli!
where they'll turn us into moles
that eat the gold dust
and spit out blood….

(quoted in Senanu and Vincent 1977, 249)

Under the apartheid regime, much of this literature written by black writers who opposed government policies was banned. Readers had few opportunities to gain insights into experiences outside those sanctioned by the dominant authorities. The school literature curriculum reflected the educational philosophy of Christian National Education, established by the Nationalist government in 1948 when apartheid officially came into existence. This philosophy of education, which was still in force in the 1970s when I was teaching and continued through the 1980s, supported the teaching of colonial novels such as those written by R.M. Ballantyne (*Coral Island*), John Buchan (*Prester John*), and Henry Rider Haggard (*King Solomon's Mines*). A few lines from Buchan's 1910 novel, *Prester John,* epitomize this philosophy:

I knew then the meaning of the white man's duty. He has to take all of the risks, recking nothing of his life or his fortunes and well content to find his re- ward in the fulfilment of his task. That is the difference between white and black, the gift of responsibility, the power of being in a little way a king, and so long as we know this and practise it, we will rule not in Africa alone but wher- ever there are dark men who live only for the day and for their bellies. (264)

These texts were read uncritically, with little effort to put them in a historical perspective or to challenge the racist and imperialist prejudices they promote. Perhaps one way for students to have resisted the ideology of such texts would have been to offer them antiracist literature with the potential to uncover the culturally loaded metaphors of colonial novels and to expose their gaps and silences. As the South African writer Njabulo Ndebele (1994) explains, much of the resistance literature written by black South Africans during the apartheid era served to "unmask" official government policy and institutionalized prejudice:

> We are confronted by so many surfaces in our day-to-day lives. So many masks. Writing enables us to crack the surface and break through to the often deliberately hidden essence. What we find may either bring joy, or sadness, hope or despair, but almost always yields insight. It is this masking and un-masking that often constitutes the terrain of conflict between the writer and of-ficial culture. Writers strive to remove the blanket which officialdom insists on spreading and laying over things. (12)

Many white writers also engaged in resistance writing and consequently suffered from this same government blanketing. Nadine Gordimer (1995), who was co-leader of the Congress of South African Writers with Ndebele, describes her efforts to become part of the society in which she lived and wrote:

> Without my making any display of political commitment, my writing became the "essential gesture" of the writer to her or his society of which Roland Barthes speaks. It was with my stories and novels, my offering of what I was learning about the life within me and around me, that I entered the commonal-ity of my country....As a consequence, some of my books were banned. (132)

All this is history and much has changed in the democratic South Africa with integrated schools and new curricula. For the past few years, Nadine Gordimer has been able to speak of South Africa as "my country," and to claim, "I am no longer a colonial," and black African writers and readers are able to gain emotional and imaginative access both to their own and to others' experiences in poetic fictions that resonate with their lives. Sipho Sepamla (1982) reflects on the importance of such imaginative experiences in his own way when he writes:

> I was brought up on Shakespeare, Dickens, Lawrence, Keats and other English greats. True enough, they opened my eyes, they gave me inspiration. In short, I received a rich sustenance from these men. But for my body to have remained healthy, for my eyes to have kept me on the right course I would have liked to have laid my hands on the "unrewarding rage" of Richard Wright, James

Baldwin, Leroi Jones and other Afro-American writers. These men I would
have liked tenfold because they have all sucked from the tits of my mother.
(116)

Sepamla's words are a reminder that to discover who we are as readers
and as writers we need access to literature that speaks to our own diverse
cultural experiences. A sense of place is located at the heart of a writer's
very being. Yet to write and to read only from a "local habitation" may
be to write and read from a self-obsession that serves to deny the power
of the imagination. When writers write only from their own experiences
and point of view, they belie the very nature of fiction. As Nadine
Gordimer (1995) reflects,

> to posit that the writer's range of imagination plays solely or mainly upon his
> own life, that the writer is imprisoned in the need to "make this intelligible,"
> that fiction is autobiography, is to deny the secret of the imagination, not to put
> it forth. Beside the proposition I would place Toni Morrison's statement: "The
> ability of writers to imagine what is not the self...is the test of their power."
> (14)

For readers of fiction, such a maxim is also true. My white middle-class
South African students were denied not only the experience of reading
literature that resonated with their own experiences of living within a rich
multicultural milieu but also the opportunity to read texts that illuminated
the lives of their peers of other races and cultures. As we journey
imaginatively through uncharted territory, we come to realize that we create
the road as we walk along it together with others. We begin and move from
where we are, we chart a course, but there is no certain destination, and the
complexities of virtual experiences are rarely anticipated. As Trinh Minh-ha
(1994) says, the power of story lies in its ability to move the limits of what
we experience, what we know:

> Journeying across generations and cultures, tale-telling excels in its powers of
> adaptation and germination; while with exile and migration, travelling ex-
> panded in time and space becomes dizzyingly complex in its repercussive ef-
> fects. Both are subject to the hazards of displacement, interaction and
> translation. Both, however, have the potential to widen the horizon of one's
> imagination and to shift the frontiers of reality and fantasy, or of Here and
> There. Both contribute to questioning the limits set on what is known as 'com-
> mon' and 'ordinary' in daily existence, offering thereby the possibility of an
> elsewhere-within-here, or-there. (10–11)

For me as a teacher in South Africa, those powerful stories were
constrained by a British canon that appeared effortlessly to have survived a

journey of thousands of miles and to have transcended changing cultures, climates, histories, and traditions. My belief in the universality of the Western literary canon went unchallenged. More recently, I have come to believe, with critics such as Barbara Herrnstein-Smith (1984) that we confuse the fact that "texts have endured with the claim that they have some distinctive right to endure, when in fact the reasons for the endurance involve nostalgia, conservative political pressures, stock rhetorical needs, and the inertia of established power" (33). Perhaps what we really mean when we talk about universal experiences in literature are cultural responses that have been shaped by our own Western tradition. This tradition, exported by Britain to colonies across the globe, attempted to efface indigenous traditions and replace them with a literary nostalgia for daffodils, spring, and a Union Jack.

When I left South Africa in 1972 to move to Canada, apartheid was still firmly entrenched in the country, habeus corpus had been suspended, and suspected "terrorists" could be locked in prison for 180 days without any access to a lawyer or to a hearing. There was little freedom of any kind for black South Africans and few educational or employment opportunities. In this atmosphere of fear, distrust of others, and enforced segregation based on a form of racial identity, there was little optimism about any forthcoming developments in multicultural education and no likelihood of canonical reforms. It would take more than twenty years before the situation changed in that country. In Britain, the United States, and Canada, the scenario was more optimistic. Each of these countries, in separate ways, was learning how to deal with particular issues of human rights and institutional structures and beginning to acknowledge the diverse needs of its increasingly heterogeneous population. Within the framework of these political and social changes, new reading practices and new ways of thinking about literary canons were beginning to evolve.

Surveying the Scene:
International Contexts for
Multicultural Literary Education

What you chart is already where you've been. But where we are going, there is no chart yet.

Audre Lorde (1988, 130)

The new canon must become a dynamic concept, less interested in codification and more in transformation, less in pluralism and more in justice. We must admit to ourselves that the multicultural classroom and multicultural practice must be invented.

James C. Hall (1995, 6)

Maps can offer clues to paths we might follow as we attempt to explore a particular cultural space, but they cannot substitute for the experience of surveying a landscape ourselves. In my survey of the historical development of various forms of multicultural education systems in three Western countries, I consider how reading practices are embedded within community assumptions about politics, literature, and writing, and, as Ashcroft, Griffiths, and Tiffin (1989) have suggested, are "resident in institutional structures such as education curricula and publishing networks" (189).

In the United States and Canada, increasing numbers of immigrants coming from a variety of cultures in the period following the Second World War radically altered the makeup of the cultural mosaics already in existence in these countries. In Britain, a sudden increase in postwar migration from former colonies in the West Indies, India, and Africa had similar effects. All three of these Western democratic countries responded to the challenges of increasingly pluralistic societies by adopting strategies of multicultural and intercultural education. James Lynch (1986) argues that multicultural education is concerned with the educational needs of all minorities, whether recently arrived, established, or indigenous, and with the needs of majority students of both sexes as they learn how to live in harmony within a multiracial society. Multicultural education, he explains, is one major way by which these societies have attempted to reconcile the twin goals of social cohesion, which aims at the maintenance of social and political stability, and of cultural diversity, which actively encourages support for a diversity of cultures within a variety of pluralist contexts.

Western societies have adopted a variety of paradigms in constructing education systems appropriate to their own particular needs and perceptions of cultural pluralism. International influences have provided a basic ethic of humanity that has underpinned efforts to establish forms of multicultural education. The United Nations Declaration of Human Rights in 1948 set the tone for humanitarian changes to education, followed by the European Convention of Human Rights in 1950, the International Covenant on Civil and Political Rights in 1966, the UNESCO Declaration on Race and Racial Prejudice in 1978, and the Convention on the Elimination of all Forms of Discrimination Against Women in 1979. By 1983, there were over fifty of these declarations and covenants. Such agreements have identified common human rights that have provided educators with an international context for developing policies of multicultural education and have offered a moral definition for its implementation.

In addition to international agreements on human rights, Lynch (1986) believes that there are a number of crucial principles of procedure for the implementation of strategies of multicultural education. These include teacher knowledge and commitment to international and national contexts of human rights; active educational implementation strategies; re-educative approaches to racism and appropriate pedagogical strategies for prejudice reduction and elimination; an effort to achieve a balance between home and national language policies; a need for multicultural education throughout the curriculum; an understanding of differing learning styles; and the development of new and alternative means of assessment. All of the above, as Lynch suggests, imply major and fundamental reforms in teacher education.

In Britain, multicultural education has moved through a number of phases in the period following the Second World War. A "laissez-faire" attitude toward the new social phenomenon of cultural diversity lasted from the end of the war until the early 1960s and was dominated by a policy of cultural hegemony. When I lived in England in the 1950s and early 1960s, there were few people of color in the school system; society was divided primarily by entrenched notions of class. In the succeeding years, during the time I was studying and teaching in South Africa and beyond, Britain went through enormous changes with a high rate of immigration from former Commonwealth countries. In its struggle to deal with sudden cultural and linguistic diversity, Britain placed a heavy emphasis on English as a Second Language and on a dispersal policy that led to the marginalization of ethnic minorities.

By the early 1970s urgent issues of multiculturalism prompted education authorities to respond with a series of reports that pointed to the educational underachievement of immigrant children, particularly those of West Indian origin. The publication in 1985 of *The Swann Report* ("An Inquiry into the Education of Children from Ethnic Minority Groups") provided an important stimulus to developments in multicultural education and signaled an acknowledgment that racism was the most significant factor in the unequal achievement of ethnic minorities in schools. The report recommended pluralist approaches in education and the provision of equal opportunities for all students in British schools. In particular, the report stressed the need for teachers to acknowledge that education occurs in a specific historical and cultural context in which the dominant culture plays a major role in silencing minority cultures.

Joan Goody and Hugh Knight (1985), commenting on the recommendations from *The Swann Report,* suggest that three particular ideas in the report are crucial to teachers of English: the need to be sensitive to the different experiences that have shaped the individual student in the classroom; the need for antiracist classroom approaches that are consistent and longterm; and the need to acknowledge the crucial role of classroom activities, discussions, and pupil-teacher and pupil-pupil interaction:

> These are the strengths of ordinary English teaching which together with increased awareness of positive elements of linguistic and cultural diversity, and of the special responsibility and opportunities there are for English teachers to help their pupils to understand and combat racism, can make a pedagogical reality of the present thinking about pupils in our multi-ethnic society. (7)

Many teachers in Britain were encouraged by new literary resources that they hoped would widen cultural perspectives, deepen insights, and help teachers and students to understand the extent and effects of colonialism. But at the same time, these multicultural texts antagonized a number of parents and were criticized by conservative educationalists who saw visions of social disintegration and the collapse of objective standards in suggested changes to the canon of literature.

New educational policies of the Tory government in the mid-1980s worked against the implementation of recommendations from *The Swann*

Report. This government set up a number of commissions to investigate English teaching, culminating in *The Kingman Report* (*Report of the Committee of Inquiry into the Teaching of English Language* 1988) that stressed the importance of maintaining a cultural status quo in English teaching. It issued a warning that

> a generation of children may grow up deprived of their entitlement—an introduction to the powerful and splendid history of the best that has been thought and said in our language. Too rigid a concern with what is "relevant" to the lives of young people seems to pose the danger of impoverishing not only the young people, but the culture itself, which has to be revitalized by each generation. (11)

This view of literature reinforces cultural stereotypes in the belief that certain canonized texts help students to discover "universal truths" and "universal human experiences." It implies that non-European texts are by definition lacking in literary quality, that "relevant" is equated with inadequacy in literary terms. Promoters of this "high culture" define "universal human experience" in terms of their own image and consider literary merit to be confined to texts written predominantly by white Anglo-Saxon writers. Brian Cox (1992), describing the determination of many British educators to institutionalize an exclusive teaching of the "great works" of English literature, comments:

> In England the desire for an "English" tradition is said by some of its critics to hide a deep fear of our present multi-cultural society, a determination to maintain our present class structure, the existing hierarchies of power. (3)

In contrast to these concerns for maintaining a monolithic cultural heritage, many English teachers in Britain in the 1980s did acknowledge the increasing diversity of their school population by offering their students a wider range of texts and introducing strategies of an antiracist education. *English for Ages 5 to 16*, published in *The Cox Report* in June 1989, offered encouragement to these teachers by supporting the concept of reading literature from "differing cultural perspectives" (item 7.6) and stressing the virtues of "an active involvement with literature," which "enables pupils to share the experience of others" (item 7.3):

> Today, literature in English in the classroom can—and should—be drawn from different countries. All pupils need to be aware of the richness of experience offered by such writing, so that they may be introduced to the ideas and feelings of cultures different from their own. (item 7.5)

In the 1990s, English teachers in Britain who wished to teach a diverse range of literature struggled to maintain their autonomy in text selection in the face of increasingly acrimonious debates and government demands for standardized testing, with compulsory texts of largely canonical literature being mandated for certain grade levels in a National Curriculum.

Questions of cultural identity have been at the forefront of Britain's multicultural policies and have reverberated through the national imagination for the past three decades as it has become increasingly clear that Britain no longer has an empire and has become a postcolonial society. According to Catherine Hall (1996), in the mid-1990s, 6.3 percent of Britain's population was classified as ethnic minorities. In urban areas such as London and Birmingham, the number increased to over 20 percent of the population. As Hall (1996) explains,

> The legacy of the British Empire is immediately visible in contemporary Britain....The decolonised peoples of Jamaica, Trinidad, Barbados, Guyana, India, Pakistan, Bangladesh and other once colonies of the Empire who have made their home in Britain together with their children and their children's children, act as a perpetual reminder of the ways in which the once metropolis is intimately connected to its "peripheries." Both colonisers and colonised are linked through their histories, histories which are forgotten in the desire to throw off the embarrassing reminders of Empire, to focus instead on the European future. (67)

Britain still has a long way to go in rethinking what its agenda might be in the context of what Hall calls a "post-nation," a society that is able to discard notions of "a homogenous nation state with singular forms of belonging" (67) and move toward a new understanding of a contemporary heterogeneous Britain that is linked in a web of connections with people across Europe and the globe.

Many immigrants to Britain have had great adjustments to make in adapting to a new environment, in dealing with conflicting expectations, and in many cases coping with racism and prejudice. I have been an immigrant myself, moving to three different countries in different continents at three different times in my life. Largely because I am white and middle-class, I have been able to enter these different countries with a sense of privilege, with a feeling of being "valued," and my educational experiences have generally been positive. This has not been the case for many immigrants of color. For example, Suzanne Scafe (1989) speaks of her experiences of moving from Jamaica to London in the mid-1970s and choosing to study black American literature and history at one of the new British "progressive" universities. She had great hopes that her previously positive reading experiences with authors such as James Baldwin would be enriched in a university classroom context, but she was quickly disillusioned:

> What happened, of course, was that the experience that I'd had of reading about Black lives—not Othello or other heroic figures of a white consciousness and a racist culture, but as they're lived—was shattered by the tools of literary criticism and a hostile literary establishment. There was something devastating about seeing or listening to texts in which I felt implicated, destroyed by the dry cutting tones of an English seminar....Our vulnerability (there were two of us) as young, alienated Black students, who did not have the brittle confidence others had acquired in public schools, was exploited. We were expected to attend and even to confer credibility on these dubious proceedings. (5–6)

After her alienating experiences at university, Scafe began teaching at a Further Education College with a high proportion of black students. There, she came to understand that schools "transmit the notion, passed off as truth, that culture is white, male and middle-class" (23) and that, consequently, her black students did not expect to see aspects of their own culture reflected in the curriculum. Her experiences of introducing black literature into the classroom led her to caution that so-called black culture is not a unified whole, but is complex and contradictory. Teachers of literature by black authors, she continues, need to realize that expressions of diverse cultural forms cannot be grafted onto an unchanged curriculum unless a historical and political context is provided for those forms. Scafe's experiences, both as a student reading black literature in predominantly white classes and as a teacher of black literature to black students, offer interesting dual perspectives on the complexities of multicultural literary education. She highlights some of the dilemmas that face teachers in other Western countries who are attempting to offer more pluralistic approaches to multicultural text selection and teaching:

> To introduce Black literary texts into the classroom without being aware of some of the contradictions of a culture and its production, and some of the complex feelings students have in relation to it, creates problems. The potential the school may have to devalue the texts and their reading merely reinforces students' feelings about otherness and may confirm their sense of the superiority of the dominant culture. Black literature as an oppositional cultural form cannot be taught alongside traditional literature in a way which leaves the cultural assumptions uncontested. It has to be used to question those assumptions, and in order to do this effectively Black literature must be taught in the context of a completely revised approach to English teaching. (25)

Scafe (1989) includes in her discussion of teaching black literature the voices of two of her black students, Kehinde and Jumoke, speaking about their different experiences in English classes. Responding to the suggestion that more black literature should be included in the curriculum, Kehinde stresses the positive value of reading these texts and their benefit in showing people that black literature has an important place in society in Britain.

Jumoke, her classmate, in response to the same question, is more skeptical:

> I get fed up with it really. I didn't really come to college for that. Some of it's all right....The thing is, though, it doesn't get you anywhere, does it? I mean we listen to music and we did some of those poets. It's not really English though, is it? I've never seen an exam in it anyway. (10)

These comments illuminate the need for teachers to reexamine a multicultural and antiracist pedagogy in order to discover why some students like Jumoke feel compromised and resentful, and to challenge the assumption that merely adding on a few multicultural literary texts to an otherwise unchanged curriculum will be enough to confirm their importance.

The experiences of Suzanne Scafe and her black students resonate with the experiences of minority and immigrant peoples in other Western countries. In the United States, for example, African-Americans, Native Americans, and other marginalized groups have long experiences of being erased from canonized texts and from the dominant culture, although this situation has recently shown signs of changing. Historically, the United States has moved from a "melting pot" mentality, which sought to assimilate all children into a homogenized American culture, toward what has been described as a "salad bowl" perspective, wherein each group reflects both its unique sense of identity and its American experience. In schools, this shifting point of view has encouraged teachers to move away from a view of diversity as "cultural deficit," which implied that students needed to become more compatible with the American school system, toward a "culturally different" perspective, which views plurality as enriching the classroom and sees individuals as unique.

The struggle for civil rights among black people in the United States has been long and bitter. The crucial Supreme Court ruling in *Brown vs. Board of Education of Topeka* in 1954, which declared the segregation of black and white children in school to be illegal, was the turning point in the civil rights movement. In the following years, several civil rights acts sought to end years of discrimination against people of color. Similarly, the struggle for acceptance of literary works by people of color in the United States has also been fought in ongoing debates. A little over a decade ago, Toni Morrison (1989) summarized the argument over the "quality" of minority literature, which she claimed was being used to disguise the political interests of the dominant discourse:

> A powerful ingredient in this debate concerns the incursion of third-world or so-called minority literature into a Eurocentric stronghold....From the seventeenth century to the twentieth, the arguments resisting that incursion have marched in predictable sequence: (1) there is no Afro-American (or thirdworld) art, (2) it exists and is inferior, (3) it exists and is superior when it measures up to the "universal" criteria of Western art, (4) it is not so much "art" as ore-rich ore—that requires a Western or Eurocentric smith to refine it from its "natural" state into an aesthetically complex form. (6)

The effects of such exclusions of minority literatures from the Anglo-American literary canon have been devastating for people of color throughout the United States. In 1955, African-American writer James Baldwin described how he was made to feel "a kind of bastard of the West" as he read canonized authors whose works did not relate to any of his own history:

> I might search in them in vain forever for any reflection of myself. I was an interloper; this was not my heritage. Still at the same time, I had no other heritage which I could possibly hope to use—I had certainly been unfitted for the jungle or the tribe. I would have to appropriate these white centuries. I would have to make them mine—would have to accept my special attitude, my special place in this scheme—otherwise I would have no place in any scheme. (101)

In hauntingly similar terms, Laurence Yep (1987), a Chinese-American writer, related what it was like to try to build a "Chinese sense of reality" as background for writing *Dragonwings,* his novel about Chinese immigrants in turn-of-the-century California published in the 1970s:

> I felt very much like the Invisible Man, without form and without shape. It was as if all the features on my face had been erased and I was just a blank mirror reflecting other people's hopes and fears. And if I wanted to see any features on my face, I would have to go through a Hollywood prop room and go digging around for masks. (495)

Arthur Applebee's surveys on literary genres taught in high schools, conducted in 1989 and 1990, showed that at the time, only 7 percent of all literary texts used in schools were written by nonwhite authors. Applebee (1993) found that the lists of most frequently required books and authors were dominated by white males, with little change in overall balance from similar lists twenty-five or eighty years ago. As Applebee explains, "the changes that have taken place in the curriculum have hardly been sufficient to reflect the multicultural heritage of the United States" (193). Applebee concluded that as long as these texts remain unchanged, minority authors would continue to be at the margins of the culture that is legitimized by its place in the schools.

The situation for many minority writers and readers of literary texts in Canada is similar to that of minorities in the United States. Canada's efforts at multicultural education initiatives also reflect some of the same concerns as those seen south of the border: coming to terms with a need to acknowledge the claims of indigenous inhabitants and making provisions for an increasingly pluralistic immigrant population. In addition, Canada's initiatives have been guided by themes of bilingualism and the safeguard of heritage languages, attempting to reconcile the maintenance of British and French cultures with an added commitment to the numerous other cultural groups in the country.

Tension between cultural pluralism on the one hand and nationalism on the other, which appears to underlie the rhetoric of multiculturalism in Canada, has led to overlapping perspectives in multicultural school policies. Augie Fleras and Jean Leonard Elliot (1992) identify these policies as "compensation," "enrichment," "enhancement," and "empowerment" (190). The first approach is similar to Britain's "assimilationist" policy of attempting to integrate immigrant students into the established norms of the school classroom. The second approach, "enrichment," encourages all students to "celebrate diversity" as they study facts about different cultures and sample ethnic foods in an effort to foster social harmony. This model, as Fleras and Elliot suggest, risks pushing diversity to the margins as a "decorative tile in an essentially mainstream curriculum" (191).

An "enhancement" model takes a more critical approach to multiculturalism by exploring the processes that hinder the success of marginalized groups in schools and considering the dynamics of power relations. This model interrogates the system's complicity in ethnic and racial discrimination and attempts to raise these issues in classroom discussions. The approach leads into an "empowerment" model, which demands a proactive, antiracist education in order to establish education for equity and to restructure the education system to allow marginalized groups to succeed on their own terms. Many educators argue that despite "official" policies of multiculturalism that have been mandated at both federal and provincial levels, changes have been "ideological rather than structural" (Alladin 1992, 80) and schools continue to function largely as assimilationist agencies.

There has also been widespread criticism of Canada's official multicultural policies, both from right-wing conservative activists who believe multiculturalism is an assault on a supposedly "pure" form of Canadian culture, and from some members of minority groups who fear that multiculturalism fosters a superficial tolerance of plurality rather than a true acceptance of diversity. Canadian writer Neil Bissoondath, for example, in an article in *The Globe and Mail* (January 28, 1993) complained that multiculturalism "has highlighted our differences rather than diminished them." This policy, he believes, "has led to the institutionalizing and enhancement of a ghetto mentality," leading to "a divisiveness so entrenched that we face a future of multiple solitudes with no central notion to bind us" (A17). In his subsequent best-selling book, *Selling Illusions: The Cult of Multiculturism in Canada* (1994), Bissoondath made similar arguments:

> I have lived in Canada for over twenty years, longer than I have lived anywhere else. I have built a life and a career here. I know who I am, know my autobiography, am at ease with it. But I also know that the specifics of my personality did not freeze, upon my arrival in Toronto, into a form suitable for multicultural display....To pretend that one has not evolved, as official multiculturalism so often seems to demand of us, is to stultify the personality, creating stereotype, stripping the individual of uniqueness: you are not yourself, you are your group. It is not really a mosaic that one joins—the parts of a mosaic fit neatly together, creating a harmonious whole—but rather a zoo of exoticism that one enters. (211)

While Bissoondath argues for a liberal nonracialist policy, other writers with different views have also critiqued Canada's efforts to introduce official multicultural policies, claiming that these have been ineffectual in bringing about real changes. Marlene Nourbese Philip (1992), for example, promoting a much stronger antiracist policy, argues that institutional and educational discrimination against visible minorities has not been addressed by official multiculturalism: "The currents of racism in Canadian society run deep, they run smooth, lulling white Canadians into a complacency that will see racism anywhere else but in Canada" (12).

The views of writers as distinct as Bissoondath and Nourbese Philip suggest that the debate over how to foster a Canadian society that values heterogeneity and diverse cultures and works successfully to eliminate racism is far from over. Even related questions about how to define what constitutes Canadian literature have been argued about over the years. In the 1970s, Robert Kroetsch wrote that the "Canadian writer's particular predicament is that he works with a language within a literature, that appears to be his own," but that concealed in the word "Canadian" is "other experience, sometimes British, sometimes American" (quoted in Ashcroft, Griffiths, and Tiffin 1989, 45). Margaret Atwood, in her discussion of Canadian literature, *Survival* (1972), considered that most Canadian writers "share a pervasive interest in the myths of identity and authenticity and a profound sense of alienation produced by displacement" (17). Fifteen years later, Milan Dimic (1988) suggested that often the first insight about Canadian literature at which scholars and critics alike arrive is "that there is no such thing" (144) and that most Canadian immigrant literature was being ignored. A later essay on so-called "minority" literatures by Ranu Samantrai (1995) reformulates the same question, as she ponders the increasing ambiguities of defining writers as Canadian. Questions of canonicity, about the Canadian nation, about immigration and multiculturalism, Samantrai claims, are all intertwined. She uses the case of Rohinton Mistry to illustrate her point:

> He is by ethnicity a Parsi, by national origin an Indian, and by residence a Canadian. Mistry's work has been acknowledged as legitimately Canadian by no less an authority than the committee that grants the Governor General's Awards, Canada's highest literary prize. *Such a Long Journey,* a novel about Parsis in Bombay, was the recipient of this honour; it was also short-listed for Britain's Booker Prize. Only those who promote a cynical nationalism would deny Mistry's work the status of Canadian literature. Yet its inclusion in that category has a paradoxically double effect. On the one hand, insisting on Mistry's location within Canada confirms the nation as the natural entity capable of generating ways of being and thinking, understood in such homogenizing phrases as "the national character." On the other, that strategic insistence serves to explode the very idea of Canada, impossibly stretching its boundaries to include places, people, and memories conventionally excluded from the Canadian mainstream. The fact that Mistry's work is also claimed by Indians as Indian fiction and by Parsis as Parsi fiction suggests a breakdown and an overlap of nations such that it is unclear where India ends and Canada begins. (34)

Samantrai's point is, I believe, valuable for an understanding both of the current scene of Canadian literature and of issues of canonicity. Instabilities of boundaries, issues of migrancy, considerations of plural identities, all of which argue against notions of authenticity, are crucial to my idea of re-mapping literary worlds in order to begin a more critical valuation of the heterogeneous cultures that comprise Canada.

Patrick Dias (1992b), commenting on the concern of many Canadian educators that our students will no longer be introduced to a "core literary culture," questions why teachers are searching for a static body of content to transmit to students. "If it is to ensure a basic cultural homogeneity across Canada and a continuous link with our past," he writes, "we need to ask ourselves how we determine what belongs and what does not belong in that cultural base?" He cautions: "Clearly, there is no static cultural base, and we cannot cling on to the old titles simply because we believe there is some intrinsic merit in them" (16).

In most Canadian provinces, even in the twenty-first century, many high school teachers cling to the "old titles," predominantly British or

American literary texts that they feel are "tried and tested" in the classroom, with multiple copies readily available in school stockrooms. Twenty years ago, Priscilla Galloway's (1980) study of the English curriculum in Ontario found that the literary selections were sexist and un-Canadian. Many of the titles listed by Galloway closely resembled those identified by Applebee's studies as popular teaching texts in the United States during the late 1980s, with Shakespeare, Dickens, Steinbeck, and Orwell among the most favored authors and Harper Lee as the more recently favored female addition. Since then, Canadian teachers have debated the merits of including more Canadian texts into their curricula, and a number of provinces have mandated that the high school curriculum should include a proportion of Canadian titles. Yet these changes have not always been well received by teachers. Robert Cameron's (1989) study of the literature being taught in Alberta high schools discovered that most teachers in his survey were teaching less than the mandated percentage of Canadian texts; teachers felt they were unfamiliar with much of this literature, that they had inadequate school resources and too little preparation to teach the texts. Only teachers who had taken university courses in Canadian literature were generally more positive about including these texts into their curricula. A decade later, a study of grade 10 English classes in Edmonton (Altmann, Johnston, and Mackey 1998) did show a marked increase in the number of Canadian texts taught at this grade level, particularly short stories by Alice Munro, Hugh Garner, and Margaret Laurence, and poems by Alden Nowlan, Raymond Souster, and Earle Birney. But teachers' selections were still overwhelmingly dominated by the same traditional Western texts identified in Galloway's (1980) study.

Text selection is inextricably linked with teachers' goals for the reading of literature in high schools. Arthur Applebee (1993) reported that teachers in his case-study schools (which included both public and private schools across the country) were concerned primarily with literary analysis of texts, with appreciation of literature, and with an understanding of literary heritage. Six percent of teachers also included exam preparation as an important goal; only half that number (three percent) expressed a concern for ethnic and gender awareness. Although there are no comparable widespread studies in Canada, high school English teachers in a small study in one Western Canadian school (Johnston and Mangat, 2002) indicated a preference for continuing to teach the same texts that appear on school reading lists throughout North America. Their concerns were focused on literary analysis of these texts in order to ensure that their students were well prepared for provincial examinations. Eaglestone (2000), discussing the entrenched nature of the high school literary canon in many Western countries, suggests another reason for this lack of variety:

> In English at all levels, the same canonical texts come up again and again, year after year. A person who studied English and has become a teacher often teaches the texts she or he was taught, in part because she or he was taught that these texts were the most important. (56)

English teachers in Canada, Britain, and the United States continue to search for ways to recognize the increasing diversity of the students in their classrooms. Yet many are uncertain about how to begin to make changes in their teaching. Official policies of multiculturalism, issues of human rights, and antiracist teaching philosophies have increased teachers' awareness that changes need to be made, but these policies have done little to help teachers to understand how complex questions of representation are intertwined with issues of culture, race, gender, and ethnicity or to comprehend what it means to initiate new reading practices in their schools.

Sites of Representation:
Culture, Race, Gender, and Ethnicity

I've always been curious about this very human thing we do which is to seek definitions. Ethnicity is a definition. We can view something when we put it within that boundary. It's inevitable that we have these definitions put on us like different articles of clothing. Ethnicity is something that got put into me by the country.

Joy Kogawa (quoted in Hutcheon and Richmond 1990, 95)

Writing is, after all, an open conversation. Works find each other. They live in the same world. The narrative of race is embedded in all narratives. My uncle loved James Baldwin at the same time he loved Lawrence Durrell. At once he cut his hair and dressed like Sam Cooke, then he enforced the proper use of English and berated the use of the demotic. So, you see, reading is full of complications.

Dionne Brand (2001, 128)

The term "site of representation" is ambiguous, implying both the geographical place to be represented and the site from which the representation emanates, whether that site is geographical, cultural, political, or theoretical. As James Duncan and David Ley (1993) suggest, once we move away from a belief that we can "simply open our eyes and see an unmediated world that yields its secrets to our gaze" (39), we begin to acknowledge that any attempt to represent the nature of other places and other people necessarily involves a form of ideological distortion that operates in the service of power. Historically, such distortions involved European travelers classifying cultures around the world into hierarchies that ranged from primitive to modern. Continents such as Africa were portrayed as comparatively "empty" lands of savagery, with the few Europeans seen as isolated representatives of reason and order. In the contemporary world, as Duncan and Ley explain, travelers and ethnographers often claim that linguistic and photographic rhetorical devices allow people who are being studied to "speak for themselves and show themselves as they really are" (43). There is little understanding that such attempts at mimetic representations are still filtered through a discourse of personal interests and relations of power.

Similarly, when we speak of issues of representation in the context of literary education, we need to look beyond the presence or absence of "positive" images of minority or "third world" people in literary texts toward the question of how social power operates in cultural and ideological practices in schools and how we call attention to complex relationships between culture, knowledge, and power. As Cameron McCarthy and Warren Crichlow (1993) point out: "Issues of identity and representation directly raise questions about who has the power to define whom, and when, and how" (xvi).

Throughout history, issues of subjectivity and identity have been intertwined with varied understandings of the word "culture." In his dictionary of social and cultural terms, *Keywords* (1976), Raymond Williams lists "culture" as one of the two or three most complicated words in the English language, partly because of its intricate historical development in several European languages, but mainly because it is used for important concepts in several distinct intellectual disciplines and in several incompatible systems of thought.

Originating from the Latin *colere,* the word "culture" has historically had a range of meanings: to inhabit, to cultivate, to protect, and to honor with worship. In its early uses it was a noun of process, concerned with the tending of crops or animals. From the sixteenth century it was also used metaphorically to indicate a process of human development. By the late eighteenth century the metaphor was used habitually to denote a general social process. Milton used it to denote a form of civility, and in the writings of Wordsworth and Jane Austen it acquired definite class associations. By the nineteenth century the word centered on the ideas of "civilization" and "progress," used to emphasize national and traditional cultures in opposition to the "mechanical" character of industrial development, and to distinguish between "human" and "material." It was also used to describe the works and practices of intellectual and artistic activity.

The nineteenth-century view of culture, epitomized by Matthew Arnold's (1981) linking of "culture" with "aesthetic" and with class distinction and claims to superior knowledge, has been steadily eroding. From the late twentieth century to the present, culture has more often been viewed as having a constituting role in human life by rendering meaning public and shared. As Jerome Bruner (1990) suggests, "Our culturally adapted way of life depends on shared differences in meaning and interpretation" (13). A culture, he believes, is constituted by commitments to particular ways of life with particular communal values that locate a people in a culture and become incorporated in their self-identity. The literature and stories of a community also participate in culture formation by affirming certain values and excluding others.

Many contemporary theorists such as James Clifford (1992) consider culture in terms of politics rather than of inheritance, with a focus on the construction and representation of culture and identity. Clifford suggests that "cultural/political identity is a processual configuration of historically given elements—including race, culture, class, gender, and sexuality" (116). Culture in this view is seen as both a signifying system and a system of material production that includes, as David Goldberg (1993) explains, "ideas, attitudes and dispositions, norms and rules, linguistic, literary, and artistic expressions, architectural forms and media representations, practices and institutions" (8) that frame and constitute a way of life.

Historically, when culture has been linked with race, class, gender, and other forms of social identity, it has tended to be asserted with visible self-assurance, confidence, and power, as was the case in apartheid South Africa. Increasingly, however, the uncertain and ambiguous nature of culture's link with race, class, and gender is being acknowledged, and racial identities in particular are seen as developing in a social context marked by uncertainty. Goldberg explains:

> Since its inception at the turn of the fifteenth century, race has emerged as an identity of anonymity, identifying social subjects conceived by modernity (and so self-conceived) as radically individualized. Race extends a tremulous identity in a social context marked by uncertainty—the uncertainty of a future beyond this life, the uncertainty of situatedness, or at least of its lack, and the uncertainties of self-assertion and assertiveness in a world of constant flux, power shifts, neighbors and nations next door one day and gone the next. Identities like race, especially of race, offer a semblance of order, an empowerment, or at minimum an affectation of power. (210)

The history of racial exclusions has been enabled by the embedding of racialized distinctions into ordinary processes of reasoning and into various conceptions of morality. A scientific cloak of "racial knowledge" provides a formal character and seeming universality to racial identity, imparting authority and legitimation to it. When race is seen as a basic categorical object, it becomes an exercise in power through the dual practices of naming and evaluating. As Goldberg explains: "In naming or refusing to name things in the order of thought, existence is recognized or refused, significance assigned or ignored, beings elevated or rendered invisible" (150). People named as the racial Other lose all autonomy and power. Production of social knowledge about those designated as Other establishes a set of guiding ideas and principles about their behavior and predictions of their likely responses. These sets of representations become stereotypes, which eventually are seen by people in power as "natural." Those rendered Other are then excluded from selfhood, and by definition from political (self-) representation. According to Goldberg (1993), "The universal claims of Western knowledge, then, colonial or postcolonial, turn necessarily upon the deafening suppression of its various racialized Others into silence" (151).

Contemporary cultural critics have moved the focus away from an essentialist view of culture that seeks to identify organic and "natural" centers of culture, toward looking at culture and identity in terms of travel relations. Such a view acknowledges the hybrid nature of most of the world's population and recognizes that there is no politically innocent methodology for cultural interpretation. James Clifford (1992) explains that although we need some strategy of localization if significantly different ways of life are to be represented, we need to ask the following questions: "How is significant difference politically articulated, and challenged? Who determines where (and when) a community draws its lines, names its insiders and outsiders?" (97). Such questions encourage us to look at culture in terms of local/global historical encounters, and to consider the specific dynamics and interplay of "native" cultural experiences with those of the intercultural traveler.

For people struggling to establish a sense of identity, a voice, and a political and cultural place, a sense of being and belonging is often perceived as moving beyond considerations of race and ethnicity to include gender, language, and art. For example, black literature, music, and culture attest to this effort at "representing" a particular autonomous sense of black identity. As Chambers (1994a) cautions, however, any search for an ethnic essence runs the risk of restricting the notion of self to a particular kind of "authenticity" that is ultimately unattainable:

> A confinement to an ethnic essence can only involve a story that cannot contemplate the excess of meaning that challenges unicity and permits differences to be. For most white people this is translated into the mirrored comfort of reflecting the universal; for those designated "black," it is taken up and translated into the troublesome specificity of a "minority" question: "an object in the midst of other objects." In the attention devoted to the margins the power being exercised at the centre is invariably obscured. For the very idea of ethnicity is used only to refer to 'minority groups' and never to white power and hegemony. So the "minority" spokesperson is expected to speak in the terms of the ethnic group, restricted to the black "community," while the white writer, artist or film maker is left free to speak about everything. (38–39)

Chambers (1994a) suggests that a questioning of ethnic and cultural essences allows for more diverse stories to emerge and "forcefully underlines the idea that ethnicity does not simply belong to the 'other,' but is also part of being white" (39). Such questioning would include problematizing what it means, for example, to be "black," "white," "British," "European," or "Canadian" today.

Arnold Krupat (1992) offers another view of culture, suggesting that language, which has traditionally served as a major determinant of identity, might serve also as a model for culture. His ideas move away from a European and American tradition of assigning individual and group identity by "race" or "blood" toward a recognition of a person as a dialogic being. His views of language link with Bakhtin's (1981) claim that language in society is always and inevitably a plural construct. Bakhtin explains:

> Language lies on the borderline between oneself and the other. The word in language is half someone else's...the word does not exist in a neutral and impersonal language...but rather it exists in other people's mouths, in other people's contexts, serving other people's intentions; it is from there that one must take the word and make it one's own. (293)

For Bakhtin, people are dialogic beings, inconceivable without others, and a text is inherently a "heteroglossia," a crossroads of many voices. A word is seen not as something fixed, but as an intersection of textual surfaces, creating a dialogue among three voices: that of the writing subject, that of the person addressed, and that of the cultural context in which the text is both written and read. Commenting on Bakhtin's work, Guillén (1993) states:

> Thus the word, which is double, "one and other" at the same time, can be considered from a horizontal or a vertical point of view: horizontally, the word belongs equally "to writing subject and addressee"; and vertically, to the text in question and to other prior or different texts. (245)

In Bakhtin's writings, dialogue acquires a special breadth, function, and intensity that moves it from its literal meaning toward a figurative sense that encompasses both text and people. So a human being, like a text, is heterogeneous, a mixture of all kinds, endlessly engaged in a dialogue with others. People's diversity corresponds to the need for verbal expression that manifests the presence of others, the consciousness of others, and the response to the words of others. People, then, like words in a text, continually encounter and engage in dialogue with the unfamiliar, the strange, the unknown. As Bakhtin (1981) explains:

> The word, directed towards its object, enters a dialogically agitated and tension-filled environment of alien words, value judgements and accents, weaves in and out of complex interrelationships, merges with some, recoils from others, intersects with yet a third group: and all this may crucially shape discourse, may leave a trace in all its semantic layers, may complicate expression and influence its entire stylistic profile. (276)

Bakhtin's views on a dialogic approach to language and to life move beyond the polarities set up by a dialectic. They move us toward an understanding that culture, like language, is better conceptualized in dialogical rather than oppositional terms.

A dialogical approach to culture moves away from the dichotomized, binary reasoning that has traditionally served as a justification for imperial domination and that sets up a simple dichotomy of good/evil that is both reductionist and unfruitful. A dialogical approach to such issues of culture, race, and ethnicity may promote a more useful strategy of recognizing the moral and political implications of colonization and racism while acknowledging the complexities and contradictions in any discourse of good and evil.

Gayatri Spivak (1988), seeking a radical restructuring of the traditional perspectives, norms, and assumptions of Western thought, also argues against a dialectical approach to culture. She suggests that it is not enough simply to produce alternative or counter-histories to Western histories but that there is a need to contest the far-reaching implications of the systems of which they form a part. To this end, Spivak seeks to produce a new narrative of how the "Third World" was itself created as a set of representations, not only for the West but also for the colonized people being represented. As Robert Young (1990) explains, Spivak believes that imperialism is concerned not only with land and with economy, but also with constituting subjects whom she calls "subalterns." Her aim is to reorient subaltern history away from a simple retrieval of a person's consciousness and voice toward an understanding of how class and gender intersect with race/ethnicity to create complex and heterogeneous subject positions. Such heterogeneity speaks against notions of an undifferentiated colonial subject or subaltern. As a "Third World" woman herself, living and working in the American academy, Spivak struggles against such homogeneity. Relating her ideas particularly to the position of "Third World" women, Spivak claims that as a woman, the subaltern "cannot speak" because everyone else speaks for her, so she cannot be heard by the privileged of either the First or Third Worlds, but is continuously rewritten as the object of imperialism or patriarchy. For Spivak, there is no "authentic" voice to be recovered out of the imposed silence of history.

Any attempt to dialogize dominant monologues recognizes that dialogue is not an abstract ideal but is present everywhere in society. Dialogue encourages the view that changes in society, in canons, and curricula may emerge from the deconstruction of all essentialist notions of the us/them and West/rest type. Bakhtin's notion of heteroglossia, applied to concepts of culture, race, and ethnicity, encourages plurality and diversity. It moves us away from the romanticized view that has used ethnicity as a parochial slogan to mask real issues of race and power.

For many colonized peoples, emerging as they were from years of subjugation and silencing, it was reassuring to think of cultural identity in terms of a shared, collective "one true self" that was "out there" waiting to be unearthed and brought to light once colonization had come to an end. Such a concept of cultural identity played a crucial role in postcolonial struggles throughout the world, and it shaped the writing of poets such as Aimé Césaire and Leopold Senghor. Franz Fanon (1963) described this desire for a rediscovery of identity as "directed by the secret hope of discovering beyond the misery of today, beyond self-contempt, resignation and abjuration, some very beautiful and splendid era whose existence rehabilitates us both in regard to ourselves and in regard to others" (170).

A more contemporary view of cultural identity in the postcolonial context acknowledges that there are always critical points of difference, of rupture and discontinuity in any consideration of "who we are." Such a position recognizes that although cultural identities have histories, they are constantly undergoing transformation and are always framed by the interplay of history, culture, and power. Difference lives alongside continuity and continually forms and transforms cultural identity. This postmodern view of cultural identity is often more troubling for many postcolonial people, who see themselves as being represented as "Other" in the texts of the European colonizers but who are unable to speak for themselves from any transparent sense of "true identity." They become trapped in what Homi Bhabha (1986) has called "the ambivalent identifications of the racist world" (xv). Yet such hybridity may also be liberating and energizing, as people move away from a view of an essentialist identity toward a new form of ethnicity that is heterogeneous and diverse, and creates new places from which to speak. This creative hybridity has been increasingly evident in the texts of contemporary postcolonial writers such as Salman Rushdie, Gabriel García Márquez, Amy Tan, Toni Morrison, and Wayson Chow. Similarly, hybridity links with dialogism in allowing those labeled as the "evil colonizers," and others, such as white academics who are linked to the colonizers by virtue of race, class, or gender, to recognize differences and similarities as intersecting pathways that may lead to creative possibilities for new understandings.

The Last "Post"? Postcolonialism and Literary Education

All this fuss over Empire—what went wrong here, what went wrong there— always makes me quite crazy, for I can say to them what went wrong: they should never have left their home, their precious England, a place they loved so much, a place they had to leave but could never forget. And so everywhere they went they turned it into England; and everybody they met they turned English. But no place could ever really be England, and nobody who did not look exactly like them would ever be English.

Jamaica Kincaid (1988, 24)

I think those of us who teach "postcolonial" literatures should at least point out the absurdity of our being saddled with the responsibility of teaching about two-thirds of the world that our institutional position forces us into. And we should stop making and accepting homogenizing theories that create a "unitary" field out of such disparate realities.

Arun Mukherjee (1998, 223)

In a very fundamental sense, the term "postcolonial" refers to that which has been preceded by colonization. Yet this literal definition does little to explain the complexity of the term as it used by postcolonial theorists or to clarify the ideological content of the term. Part of the confusion, Arif Dirlik (1994) explains, stems from the use of the term "postcolonial" both as a description of global conditions after colonialism and "as a description of a discourse on the above-named conditions that is informed by the epistemological and psychic orientations that are products of those conditions" (332). Dirlik suggests that one does not have to be literally postcolonial to share in the themes common to much postcolonial discourse.

Deepika Bahri (1995) elaborates on this dual use of the term by cautioning that the notion of the "postcolonial" as a literary genre and an academic construct may have meanings quite separate from its historical groundings. She comments: "The multiplicity of meanings obliges us to confront two discomforting propositions: not only that the map is not the territory but that it is possible…that the map no longer precedes the territory" (53). Theoretical perspectives on postcolonialism, she suggests, tend to be removed from the material realities of those peoples inhabiting postcolonial societies, taking little account of their continuing economic dependence on the West.

Postcoloniality, viewed in a historical context, is integrally tied to European imperialism. For countries that were once colonized, the "post" in postcolonialism is in many ways a temporal fiction, suggesting a newly acquired state of independence into which is indelibly inscribed the trace of the imperial nation. The term "postcolonial" prevents any conception of a nation that preceded colonization. Its use has been criticized because it rejects a people's pre-national past and glosses over the realities of local cultures and social realities in favor of a concept of "nation" artificially defined by citizenship and a passport. In a metaphorical sense, the term "postcolonialism" is problematic, suggesting that countries have moved along in a linear way from a "pre-colonial" stage, through a "colonial" era and on to a "post-colonial" state. This idea of linear development ensures that the focus is always on the colonizer.

Over the past years, postcolonial discourse has attempted to address concerns about national origin by focusing more on subject-positions than on national identity. Homi Bhabha (1990) has suggested that we should move away from "metanarratives of nations" (1) that consciously or unconsciously repress knowledge of difference, and that we focus instead on the idea of transnationality, a concept that considers the potential of migrancy and hybrid identities and values the intermingling of cultures, ideas, and politics. Similarly, Rushdie (quoted in Steiner, 1995) "rejoices in mongrelisation and fears the absolutisms of the Pure" (14), and sees the migrant state not as a loss but as a source of creative newness. Other postcolonial critics are more cautious, expressing concerns that people in former European colonies who were identified by Fanon (1963) as the "Wretched of the Earth," will remain wretched under the continuing process of economic and cultural annexation by multinationals, disguised under the name of modernization and economic development.

In a more literary sense, the term "postcolonial" (both with and without a hyphen), as it is used in academic and publishing circles, once referred strictly to the literatures of former colonies, but these restrictions have begun to fade now that the labels "Commonwealth" and "Third World" have fallen into disrepute among segments of the Western academy.

Rushdie, among others, has been vociferous in criticizing the use of the term "Commonwealth literature," explaining that it has not even been clear what people have meant by the designation. In an article reflecting on his participation in a Commonwealth Literature conference in Sweden, Rushdie (1983/1992) explained:

> "Commonwealth literature," it appears, is that body of writing created, I think, in the English language, by persons who are not themselves white Britons, or Irish, or citizens of the United States of America....It is also uncertain whether citizens of Commonwealth countries writing in languages other than English—Hindi, for example—or who switch out of English, like Ngugi, are permitted into the club or asked to keep out. By now "Commonwealth literature" was sounding very unlikeable indeed. Not only was it a ghetto, but it was actually an exclusive ghetto. And the effect of creating such a ghetto was, is, to change the meaning of the far broader term "English literature"—which I'd always taken to mean simply the literature of the English language—into something far narrower, something topographical, nationalistic, possibly even racially segregationalist. (62–63)

More recently, John McLeod (2000) has commented that Commonwealth literature "was really a sub-set of canonical English literature, evaluated in terms derived from the conventional study of English that stressed the values of timelessness and universality" (14). According to McLeod, much of this literature was exciting to read and helped to depict the nations with which the texts were concerned. Yet, despite their experimental elements and local focus, these texts were not viewed as particularly radical or oppositional; nor were they seen to challenge the Western criteria of excellence used to read them. In a similar vein, some postcolonial critics have criticized the use of "Third World Literature" as one more example of a simplistic binary bifurcation between colonizer/colonized that suggests a false homogenization of formerly colonized people. Although the designation is still in evidence in some academic journals, its use is often flagged as a concern.

An early text in the field of postcolonial literary studies, *The Empire Writes Back: Theory and Practice in Post-Colonial Literatures* by Ashcroft, Griffiths, and Tiffin (1989), uses the term "postcolonial" to include "literatures of African countries, Australia, Bangladesh, Canada, Caribbean countries, India, Malaysia, Malta, New Zealand, Pakistan, Singapore, South Pacific Island countries and Sri Lanka" (2). Critics have pointed out that Ashcroft, Griffiths, and Tiffin's exclusive focus in their book on literatures in the English language raises questions similar to those asked by Rushdie about Commonwealth literatures: How do we draw distinctions between what is—and is not—postcolonial literature?

A focus on literature designated as postcolonial does not come close to explaining the diffuse nature and size of postcolonial studies today, which have evolved into a disciplinary subject and a theoretical apparatus with enormous political and ideological status. An essay by Stephen Slemon (1994) offers an overview of the far-reaching nature of postcolonial studies in the 1990s. Slemon writes:

> "Post-colonialism" as it is now used in its various fields, describes a remark-ably heterogeneous set of subject positions, professional fields, and critical en-terprises. It has been used as a way of ordering a critique of totalizing forms of Western historicism; as a portmanteau term for a retooled notion of "class;" as a subset of both postmodernism and post-structuralism (and conversely, as the condition from which those two structures of cultural logic and cultural critique themselves are seen to emerge); as the name for a condition of nativist longing in post-independence national groupings; as a cultural marker of non-residency for a Third World intellectual cadre; as the inevitable underside of a fractured and ambivalent discourse of colonialist power; as an oppositional form of "reading practice;" and—this was my first encounter with the term—as the name for a category of "literary" activity which sprang from a new and wel-come political energy going on within what used to be called "Commonwealth" literary studies. (16–17)

Here, Slemon articulates some of the difficulties that postcolonial theorists face in attempting to place a concise label on the field in which they work. Another overview of the area by Bill Ashcroft (2001) suggests that the term postcolonial studies "has expanded to engage issues of cultural diversity, ethnic, racial and cultural difference and the power relations within them, as a consequence of an expanding and more subtle understanding of the di-mensions of neo-colonial domination" (11). Perhaps one of the most pow-erful aspects of postcolonialism resides in the fact that it resists closure. Like Homi Bhabha's (1994) definition of a "Third Space" that is "unrepre-sentable in itself" (37), part of the power of postcolonialism lies in its abil-ity to draw attention to the dissonances in the discourses it lies between.

For teachers, postcolonial literary theory is often viewed as a sanction-ing of multicultural studies, and many are unaware of possible problems arising from the conflation of multicultural studies with postcolonial stud-ies. A concern expressed by such critics as Deepika Bahri (1995) is that in-terest in sanitized "multicultural" texts, studied outside their immediate frame of reference, may disguise the power relations that shape the writing of the literature. Any study of this literature may encourage only a superfi-cial interest and tolerance for diversity rather than promote a genuine inves-tigation into the complexities of other cultures. As Bahri cautions,

> The contract is a fairly simple one: a) minoritized subjects are encouraged to represent themselves and their communities, in art, literature, etc., and; b) their productions are to be accepted and disseminated, usually by "multiculturals"

and primarily through educational institutions, in a spirit of learning, tolerance, and respect. Neither is inherently damaging. The problem is that such subjects are to speak as minorities; they are to represent their communities and the victimization suffered by them in individual voices; and their texts are to be used, often solo, to "inform" students....One might ask what the academy is about when it encourages students to learn about the world, often exclusively, from token fictional texts. The odd anthologized short story by Amy Tan or Mukherjee's paperback novel, we are to assume, will educate our students in other cultures. (73–74)

Instead, Bahri (1995) writes that students should read a text "for its aesthetic as well as 'socially responsible' messages and use it to raise questions that should be central to the multiculturalist project, among them representation and the benevolent tokenization that replaces previous erasure" (74).

To Bahri's suggestion, I would add the possibility of what Gerald Graff (1990) has termed "teaching the conflicts" through joint readings of a canonized Western text with a postcolonial or contemporary text or with a "rewriting" of a canonized text. Graff has suggested that exploring these conflicts can "open up a debate over the relation between social and artistic value that has too long been brushed aside or allowed to fall between the cracks that separate literary study from history and social thought" (54). This strategy may lead to a resistant reading of the canonized text and an exploration of the dissonances and ambiguities evident in contrasting texts. Such a technique also, I believe, brings to the surface tensions over the social and political contexts of literature, which are often submerged in a classroom in an attempt to let the text speak for itself. My South African students needed just this kind of resistant reading in order to deconstruct the representations, ideologies, and the political and racial assumptions of the texts they were offered in school.

Although great strides have been made in the cultural diversification of the curriculum, particularly at the college level, this does not mean that the dilemmas over text selection and reading strategies are over. As Graff (1996) cautions, "the debates over the merits, implications, and proper strategies of diversifying the curriculum are not likely to go away" (125). Graff's point is that teachers should be turning their energies to making positive educational use of these debates by incorporating them into classrooms and embedding the teaching of literature in our theoretical differences. The ensuing debates might prove to be a positive strategy for moving beyond what Graff calls "the fight for one list of books over another list of books" (136).

James Greenlaw (1994) echoes some of Graff's concerns about the need to look beyond text selection to a consideration of the kinds of teaching strategies being used in the classroom. Postcolonial pedagogy, Greenlaw, argues, differs from prescriptive multicultural projects that aspire only to increase multicultural harmony. The imperative behind postcolonial pedagogy is to find ways to help students "deconstruct racist (mis)representations of the Other as they are found in the political, social, and cultural discourses which are inscribed within the literary texts, films, music videos, magazines, newspapers, television shows, and computer forums through which students attempt to interpret their world" (7–8). Greenlaw elaborates on his particular deconstructive stance in his work with high school students:

> If students are taught the postcolonial deconstructive strategies which they need in order to examine critically how literary representations are constructed out of multiple and conflicting discourses, then at the end of a course in multicultural literature, even if they have not become better, more tolerant citizens, they will at least have been given the opportunity to learn how and why racist stereotypical (mis)representations are produced and resisted. (8)

Similar critiques of mainstream orientations to multicultural education, by Deborah Britzman et al. (1993), focus on ways students are offered so-called "accurate" and "authentic" representations of particular cultures in the hopes that these students will automatically develop tolerant attitudes. The authors elaborate:

> These newly represented cultures appear on the stage of curriculum either as a seamless parade of stable and unitary customs and traditions or in the individuated form of political heroes modeling roles. The knowledge that scaffolds this view shuts out the controversies of how any knowledge—including multicultural—is constructed, mediated, governed, and implicated in forms of social regulation and normalization. The problem is that knowledge of a culture is presented as if unencumbered by the politics and poetics of representation. (189)

This caution against presenting multicultural literature in an unquestioning and essentialist way does not imply that the voices of the oppressed, the marginalized, and the previously silenced should not be heard, but that it is simplistic to offer students "good realism" as a response to the "bad fictions" of stereotypes. As I discussed earlier, simply presenting students with a dialectic of good/evil shuts out the complexities and contradictions of power relations and denies students opportunities for exploring the fluid boundaries between such definitions.

Territories of Desire:
Contesting Canons

Travelers with closed minds can tell us little except about themselves.
Chinua Achebe (1978, 12)

The blanks in the maps included in the journals reveal the constant selection of knowledges considered appropriate for display. They consistently efface the Aboriginal groups whom the explorers have contacted and about whom some knowledge is possessed, while carefully including locations of any white settlements.
Simon Ryan (1994, 126)

"Modern Western culture," remarks Said (1990), "is in large part the work of exiles, émigrés, refugees" (357). Canada's history, in common with that of many other Western countries, has been forged by immigrants seeking out lands and new territories, has been marked by the displacement of indigenous populations and characterized by fluctuation and discontinuity. For much of the last two centuries, the heterogeneous nature of Canada as a country has been concealed under the rubric of "two solitudes:" two European languages, French and English, and two European identities. During the past decades, however, this concealing fabric has been torn apart by the unmistakable arrival of visible minorities from China, India, the Middle East, Central and South America, Africa, and elsewhere. Canadian classrooms today reflect a racial and cultural diversity that has radically challenged any Eurocentric notions of ethnic, linguistic, or cultural absolutism

In contrast to the stability of texts from the "old order" that were traditionally taught in Canadian schools, travelers' tales speak of shifting boundaries, of the impossibilities of packaging a culture or defining an authentic cultural identity. Traveling, as Trinh Minh-ha (1994) explains, can be a "process whereby the self loses its fixed boundaries—a disturbing yet potentially empowering practice of difference" (23). Travelers, she suggests, gain three supplementary identities: "Traveling allows one to see things differently from what they are, differently from how one has seen them, and differently from what one is" (23). Many teachers in today's schools have little awareness of the rich potential of such traveling. For them, a literary curriculum is a static notion, consisting of a stack of well-used texts, usually from Britain and the United States, that they feel have stood the test of time. With little understanding of the history of such texts or the power of the literary canon, such teachers resist any notion of change.

Canonicity is not so much about texts as about status and evaluation, the criteria and standards according to which not only individual works and authors, but also entire movements and discourses themselves fall in or out of favor. It is a process in which texts, styles, and approaches are designated literary and perceived as worthy of attention, or are pushed to the margins and allowed to disappear.

The admission into the English language of the word "canon" remains obscure. Originally a Greek term, *kanon*, it was used by Alexandrian scholars in the second and third centuries to mean a "straight rod," a "ruler," or "standard." The Oxford English Dictionary published between 1884 and 1928 does not contain in its twenty-five listings any word approximating the modern meaning of an approved catalogue of books. The closest is "canon" defined as a "collection or list of books of the Bible accepted by the Christian Church as genuine and inspired." Only in the supplement in 1972 is this definition expanded to include "those writings of a secular author accepted as authentic."

Jusdanis (1991) states that a study of canonicity needs to be foregrounded by an examination of the exercise of power, the role of interest, and the dynamics of struggle, which are all crucial in its formation. Texts deemed worthy of being saved and transmitted to another generation serve as objects of criticism, enter school curricula, are included in histories of literature and are annotated in anthologies. As Gerald Bruns (quoted in Landow 1992) comments:

> A text, after all, is canonical, not in virtue of being final and correct and part of an official library, but because it becomes binding upon a group of people. The whole point of canonization is to underwrite the authority of a text, not merely with respect to its origin as against competitors in the field...but with respect to the present and future in which it will reign or govern as a binding text....From a hermeneutic standpoint...the theme of canonization is power. (149)

Before the middle of the eighteenth century, only the Greek and Latin classics and the Bible were considered as serious subjects for scholarly research and discourse. By the mid-nineteenth century, the role of literature in

Britain was considered to be the reduction of diversity and the promotion of a common set of values and a common culture. This point of view was best presented in Matthew Arnold's (1869/1981) *Culture and Anarchy,* a text that saw in literature a resistance to the anarchy of the Industrial Revolution, and that was widely influential in English classrooms around the world. The canon that emerged reflected a particular British literary heritage, with texts by Shakespeare, Pope, Milton, Goldsmith, Gray, the English Romantics, and literature considered to be easily accessible to adolescents, such as Scott's *Ivanhoe.*

Throughout the nineteenth and twentieth centuries there was a continual tug of war between the "Common Reader" at one end of the rope and a representative of the cultural elite at the other. The critic F.R. Leavis (1930) was one of the most influential proponents of cultural elitism. Over a time span of more than 30 years, he elaborated his proposals for educational reforms that would elevate the status of his small minority who were capable of "appreciating Dante, Shakespeare, Donne, Baudelaire, Conrad" and who could keep alive "the subtlest and most perishable parts of tradition" (144). Leavis's inspiration for his ordering of the canon came from T.S. Eliot, who defined the canon not as a disparate set of texts but as an order of related texts, with each work gaining meaning in relation to the others. As Samson (1992) explains, the literary canon, under Leavis's direction, expanded only enough to include some additional "worthy" Western texts selected by an elite group of critics. These texts included works by D. H. Lawrence, Dickens, and Blake, who were admitted as "worthy" successors to Shakespeare, together with selected American writers such as Cooper, Hawthorne, Melville, James, and Twain.

Leavis's contempt for the Common Reader and his reverence for a cultural elite have translated in more recent times into the promotion of "cultural literacy" as expounded by right-wing critics such as E.D. Hirsch (1987) and Alan Bloom (1987), who view pluralism as a threat to the notion of a shared national language and national culture. For canonized texts, Hirsch substitutes a definitive list of dates, names, events, and titles that Americans should know. His avowed democratic intention of providing all students access to a shared cultural legacy conceals his elitist notions of what it means to be literate. It is significant that only Hirsch's culturally literate minority are eligible to construct this list of culturally significant material and are then able to label it as "ours." Hirsch's "culturally illiterate" have no part to play in constructing such a list; they are only to be taught it.

African-American critics, such as Cameron McCarthy (1993) question the approaches of these conservative educators who claim an unambiguous Western-ness as the basis of curriculum organization and implicitly demonstrate an unease and anxiety about the question of minority identities. McCarthy (1993) claims: "There is nothing intrinsically superior or even desirable about the list of cultural items and cultural figures celebrated by traditionalists like Hirsch and Bloom" (293). The very concept of "Western" is problematic, an ideological construct infused with tensions and struggles over meaning. How can being American, or Canadian, not include indigenous people and minorities such as African-Americans, who have been in the Americas at least as long as whites? As McCarthy asks:

> How is it that the history, and writings, and culture of African-Americans are non-Western? Who is demarcating the West? Do we, for instance, want to say that Ernest Hemingway is in and Alice Walker is out? Where is the line of the Western to be drawn within the school curriculum? (294–95)

Henry Giroux (1992a) echoes McCarthy's sentiments with his belief that the defense, restructuring, or elimination of a particular canon in education can only be understood within a broader range of political and theoretical considerations. Hirsch and Bloom, he explains, represent the latest cultural offensive by the new elitists to rewrite the past and construct the present from the perspective of the privileged and the powerful. As Giroux contends, such critics "disdain the democratic implications of pluralism and argue for a form of cultural uniformity in which difference is consigned to the margins of history or to the museum of the disadvantaged" (125). From this perspective, culture is seen as "an artifact, a warehouse of goods, posited either as a canon of knowledge or a canon of information that simply has to be transmitted" and pedagogy is "something one does in order to implement a preconstructed body of knowledge or information" (125). What is at stake here, Giroux believes, is not simply the issue of bad teaching but "the broader refusal to take seriously the categories of meaning, experience, and voice that students use to make sense of themselves and the world around them" (125).

In similar terms, Toni Morrison (1989) has eloquently articulated the "invisible" presence of African-Americans that shaped so much of American life and American literature.

> Now that Afro-American artistic presence has been "discovered" actually to exist, now that serious scholarship has moved from silencing the witnesses and erasing their meaningful place in and contribution to American culture, it is no longer acceptable merely to imagine us and imagine for us. We have always been imagining ourselves. We are not Isak Dinesen's "aspects of nature," nor Conrad's unspeaking. We are the subjects of our own narratives, witnesses to and participants in our own experience, and in no way coincidentally, in the experience of those with whom we have come in contact. We are not, in fact,

"other." We are choices. And to read imaginative literature by and about us is to choose to examine centers of the self and to have the opportunity to compare those centers with the "raceless" one with which we are, all of us, familiar. (8–9)

For writers such as Morrison, it is not enough to be admitted into the halls of canonicity, as defined by a small cultural and politically powerful elite; she believes that the whole idea of canonicity needs to be deconstructed.

It is relatively easy to refute the arguments of right-wing conservatists such as E.D. Hirsch and Alan Bloom, with their obvious elitist views and definitive, prescriptive views on the values of a Western culture that is limited to a list of cultural terms and beliefs. Harold Bloom's (1994) elegiac defense of the Western canon presents a more subtle appeal to Western prejudices. Bloom expressly disassociates himself both from the "right-wing defenders of the Canon, who wish to preserve it for its supposed (and non-existent) programs for social change" (4) and from contemporary critics of the Canon, whom he dubs "the School of Resentment, who wish to overthrow the Canon in order to advance their supposed (and non-existent) programs for social change" (4).

Harold Bloom's literary canon focuses on twenty-six writers whom he considers to be "authoritative in our culture" (17). His small list of writers includes those he deems as "great" Western writers, such as Dante, Chaucer, Cervantes, Montaigne, Shakespeare, Goethe, Wordsworth, Dickens, Tolstoy, Joyce, and Proust. Bloom justifies his concept of canonical works on the basis of "aesthetic strength," which he defines as "mastery of figurative language, originality, cognitive power, knowledge, exuberance of diction" (27–28).

Of immediate concern is the male orientation of Bloom's canon. Only four of his selected twenty-six "great" authors are women. Bloom dismisses such a concern lightly, claiming that "great literature will insist upon its self-sufficiency in the face of the worthiest causes: feminism, African-American culturism, and all the other politically correct enterprises of our moment" (27). Equally frustrating is Bloom's obvious contempt for issues of culture, race, ethnicity, and class. His elitist belief is that "we need to teach more selectively, searching for the few who have the capacity to become highly individualized readers and writers. The others, who are amenable to a politicized curriculum, can be abandoned to it" (17). Aesthetic value, Bloom claims, determines the immortality of texts and "very few working-class readers ever matter in determining the survival of texts" (36). Secure in his white ivory tower of aesthetic and cognitive values with his chosen few, Bloom glances down disdainfully at a map of the Western world populated by those he discounts: feminists, people of color, Native people, the poor and disadvantaged, and an "academic rabble that seeks to connect the study of literature with the quest for social change" (26).

Toni Morrison (1989), who is one of few women writers of color afforded a place in Bloom's "Canonical Prophecies for the future," supplies perhaps the most apt response to Bloom's perspective:

> Canon building is Empire building. Canon defense is national defense. Canon debate, whatever the terrain, nature and range (of criticism, of history, of the history of knowledge, of the definition of language, the universality of aesthetic principles, the sociology of art, the humanistic imagination), is the clash of cultures. And all of the interests are vested. (8)

Edward Said has been one of the most noted contemporary critics of the canon. He shares with the "canon-busters" the view that those in the academy who teach only the European classics are tacitly suppressing literature of other cultures. In his ground breaking text, *Orientalism* (1978), Said showed how canon-building rests on a process of brilliant simplifications and dialectics, with Western critics constructing an Orientalist canon of stereotypes—"unscrupulous Arab merchants, Iranian terrorists, chanting mobs"—against which to judge the grand cultural narratives of the West. According to Said, the "Orient" has been both constructed and represented through Western ideologies and institutions:

> The Orient is not merely there just as the Occident itself is not just there either. We must take seriously Vico's great observation that men make their own history, that what they can know is what they have made, and extend it to geography: as both geographical and cultural entities—to say nothing of historical entities—such locales, regions, geographical sectors as "Orient" and "Occident" are man-made. (5)

Western writers, as well as political commentators, have taken as their starting point a fundamental division of the world into the Orient and the Occident, and developed what Gabriel (1994) terms a "collective notion of the Occidental 'us' which became integrally bound up with the idea of European superiority and various forms of Eurocentric racism" (15). This framework has allowed the construction of "otherness," a status defined in the negative, and of its flip side, the "us" or "we," whose collective national, European, Western identity rests, in part, on just such exclusions.

In a later book, *Culture and Imperialism* (1993), Said elaborates on the notion that imperial power, resistance against empire, and the production of narratives are inextricably linked:

> Stories are at the heart of what explorers and novelists say about strange regions of the world; they also become the method colonized people use to assert their identity and the existence of their own history....The power to narrate, or block other narratives from forming and emerging, is very important to culture and imperialism and constitutes one of the main connections between them. (xii–xiii)

The grand narratives of emancipation and enlightenment, Said (1993) suggests, enabled colonized people to rise up and throw off imperial subjection, and have also encouraged many people in Western countries to fight for "new narratives of equality and human community" (xiii).

Said has also supported the work of French critics such as Foucault and Derrida in their work to create a new kind of canon that operates from "nomadic centers," provisional structures that are never permanent and that offer new forms of continuity, vision, and revision. This open-ended nomadic canon espoused by Said values the potential over the institutional. His proposed world resembles what Gorak (1991) terms "a kind of mental bazaar: a place of many tongues, a variety of goods, and an endless circulation of materials and people" (215) where critics would handle the fragments of a former canon with attention and respect and then relinquish them.

The current canon debate has prompted Gorak to argue that the "Anglo-European canon, if it ever existed at all, has probably met its end. If "*canon*" suggests an unchanging, unquestioned body of received opinion, canon, in that sense, at least has permanently gone" (253). The constructed map of the Western world has shifted, has spread outwards to encompass its margins; its properties and territories have lost their center and, adrift in a turbulent sea, are floating in search of new resting places. Western culture, conceived as a protective enclosure that separates "us" from "them," has broken apart in a fragmented and hybridized world.

These changing possibilities have opened the doors for a new movement of "World Literature" that includes voices from postcolonial writers, an increasing number of women and previously marginalized writers of color from every continent. This polycultural order has redefined the canon of English literature; international writers confirm that we are living in a decentered world that allows writers and readers to discover and travel among other selves, other identities, other varieties of the human adventure. Teachers wanting to join this human adventure and to introduce new ways of reading into their classrooms seek ways to challenge the notion of a traditional Western canon of literary texts and, even more importantly, begin to examine the theoretical frameworks within which they live, read, write, and teach.

Literary Theory at the Crossroads

Teachers who denigrate theory and the need for it believe that they have got control of a discourse that has really got control of them. They become the servants rather than the masters of this discourse's ideology which they practise as though it were natural or a matter of common sense.

Jack Thomson (1992, 7)

As it stands, the concept of culture too often does the distressing sort of work that race was once used to accomplish, that is, keeping the barbarian at the gate. It happens, for example, when the literary canon is held up as proof of the West's evolution to a higher plane of existence.

John Willinsky (2001, 95)

What happens when we bring a literary text into a classroom and offer it to students to read? Margaret Mackey (1995), in her exploration of the complex relationship between readers and a literary text, emphasizes the ambiguity of trying to describe the act of reading, which is at once active and performative and yet also silent, specific, and individualistic:

> There can be few things in life more deceptive than a page of print. Black and white, fixed and stable, it mocks a reader with its definitiveness. Yet as we all know, the process of reading which begins with that page of print is by its very nature, incomplete, tentative, shifting. (2)

As Mackey explains, "Until readers learn how to imagine with words, they have missed the necessary preliminary requirement of reading fiction" (2). For teachers and students, such imaginative engagement with a literary text is an important first step for moving into a fictional world which can both inform and re-form the literary imagination, and it is a valuable prerequisite for readers to move on to deconstructing the text to interrogate its form and its ideological and political assumptions. Umberto Eco (1994) describes these levels of reading experiences metaphorically:

> There are two ways of walking through a wood. The first is to try one or several routes (so as to get out of the wood as fast as possible, say, or to reach the house of grandmother, Tom Thumb, or Hansel and Gretel); the second is to walk so as to discover what the wood is like and find out why some paths are accessible and others not. Similarly there are two ways of going through a narrative text. (27)

Reading powerful literature can, I believe, change our lives, and this experience requires the crucial first step of readers moving imaginatively into the virtual world of the text. Often, readers find it easier to move into an imaginary world when reading a book of their own choice and when there is no pressure either to complete the book or to respond to the kinds of "post-reading" questions that many teachers want their students to attend to. While acknowledging the added complexity of individual reading in a communal setting, I believe it is still possible for students to gain what Max van Manen (1985) calls the "true pedagogical value" of a literary text, which lies in the double experience it offers: "It provides me in an intimate way with a great human experience and then, as a bonus, offers me the phenomenological experience of interpreting the first one" (186).

A literary text may weave its magic through what Steiner (1995) describes as the "the honesty of the fictive lie" (119). Rushdie elaborates on this point directly in his allegorical tale, *Haroun and the Sea of Stories* (1990). He shows how Haroun's father, the great storyteller Rashid, is sought after by politicians because people have faith in what he says even though he admits that every story he tells is completely untrue. The power of story is so strong that Khattam-Shud, the "Prince of Silence and the Foe of Speech" seeks to eliminate it. Near the end of the book, Haroun and Khattam-Shud finally meet:

> "But why do you hate stories so much?" Haroun blurted out, feeling stunned. "Stories are fun."
> "The World, however, is not for Fun," Khattam-Shud replied. "The world is for controlling."
> "Which world?" Haroun made himself ask.
> "Your world, my world, all worlds," came the reply. "They are all there to be Ruled. And inside every single story, every stream in the Ocean, there lies a world, a story-world, that I cannot rule at all. And that is the reason why." (161)

The story world, as Rushdie so engagingly reminds us, has power that moves it out of the control of the writer and out of the context in which it was conceived into the larger realm of the imagination of readers, often creeping unbidden into their consciousness and subtly transforming the way they view the world and the way they act in the world. Story can achieve radical reformulations of language, form, and ideas. And, as Steiner (1995) explains, "In changing our *ideas* about the world it changes the *world*. And since the world is history, religion, political plotting, violence, and immorality, it affects all of these" (121).

This social and political force of stories, of course, as well as being a positive force, can also be dangerous, seducing readers into believing that the world inside the text is a transparent reflection of the world outside the text, insinuating its ideology into receptive minds. The stories that colonizers told of "empty continents" created a myth of a *tabula rasa* ready to be inscribed with the "discoveries" of Western travelers; colonial texts of "savages" created myths of people who needed to be civilized, and effectively silenced indigenous inhabitants. In a critical postcolonial pedagogy, the seductions of such stories need to be resisted as much as the long-silenced stories of the colonized need to be heard.

In a classroom, how students and teachers read is also determined by the theoretical framework within which they come to texts. Of course, most students (and many teachers) might claim that they have no literary theories. They find it hard to believe that when they enter a classroom they are drenched in largely unconscious cultural and epistemological assumptions. When readers approach a literary text with the intention of "letting the text speak for itself," they are inevitably encountering the text with a vast array of unexamined theoretical presuppositions and expectations.

Some teachers in schools and colleges consider reading literary texts as a form of travel in which they "cover" a "representative" sampling of literature in a particular time period, with little opportunity to reflect on the theoretical premises that determine their reading, understanding, and responses to the texts. As Douglas Lanier (1991) writes, these teachers encourage students to embark on a pedagogical version of the two-week package tour to Europe. Lanier offers his own example:

> From a speeding tour bus, we provide students with fleeting glimpses of an overly homogenized realm called "literature," whose inhabitants—John Donne, James Joyce, Flannery O'Connor, and Alice Walker—are distinguished by little more than an author's name, a headnote, and stylistic differences....What is more, our students are not called upon to examine their own critical presuppositions, to construct multiple contexts for a single text, or to recognize how different strategies of interpretation might reinforce or conflict with one another. They have, in short, little opportunity or incentive to reflect upon the theoretical premises that govern the very activity in which they are engaged. (200)

Dennis Sumara (1994) makes a similar argument about the way the high school English curriculum can easily degenerate into an uncritical "covering of material" in a limited time span:

> Do students in the secondary English classroom dwell with texts or do they merely tour through them? Are there commonplaces for interpretation created in the English classroom, or does the use of the literary text amount to a brief stop, where students rush off the bus, take a few pictures, grab a bite to eat, relieve themselves, and then rush back on the bus to await the next destination? Are English teachers tour guides? Are students' experiences in the English classroom similar to the guided tour? (107)

As Sumara suggests, many world travelers prefer the comfort of pre-booked guided tours rather than attempting "to cope with the difficulty and the ambiguity of traveling through foreign countries on one's own" (107). Yet this more daunting approach to travel and to reading texts allows us, as travelers and as readers, to live inside new experiences with eyes and ears open and to begin to acknowledge the theoretical assumptions and preconceptions we bring to new texts and experiences.

When I was a student at school in Britain, and later at university in South Africa, I took it for granted that when I read literature "for school purposes," I would be expected to consider the text alone as the sole determinant of meaning and value. Language, I was told, allows direct access to human experiences and the meanings garnered from a literary text are timeless and universal. When teachers bring postcolonial literary texts into their classrooms, they discover that it is difficult to consider the text as an object of study without some acknowledgment of the historical and political framework of the literary work. Teachers who are used to a New Critical approach to literature will need to acknowledge new ways of approaching literary texts and will be challenged to change their belief that "great literature penetrates beyond the historically and culturally specific to a realm of universal truth whose counterpart is an essentially unchanging human condition" (Dollimore 1984, 45). American New Criticism has traditionally been silent about such themes as racism, imperialism, sexism, and inequality, but eloquent about eternal values uncontaminated by history and aesthetic considerations such as symbolism and artistic structure. The high point of New Criticism's influence was the publication of W.K. Wimsatt and Munroe C. Beardsley's *The Verbal Icon* in 1954, which formulated the New Critical view of the text as essentially a verbal complex of tensions, ironies, paradoxes, and ambiguities. As a "verbal icon," the text's main reference was to itself rather than to the world outside its textual borders.

New Criticism reinforced teaching of a limited set of prescribed texts in schools and promoted a view of literature as a body of knowledge to be transmitted from teacher to students. Its influence has been inestimable throughout the English-speaking world. It helped to establish the teaching of British canonized texts in North American schools, and although enlarging this canon through the introduction of certain postcolonial writers who were considered "immature" by European definitions, it assimilated these works into a British tradition without any consideration of the cultural context of the writer. The New Critical approach thereby prevented the new texts from being seen as innovative, distinctive, or subversive of imported European values.

The influence of New Critical theory began to fade in North American educational institutions during the 1980s as new literature courses gave currency to methods of history, philosophy, and linguistics. The influence of new European theories such as structuralism and poststructuralism encouraged the idea of meaning as self-referential rather than fixed to an external reality. Structuralism, with its roots in the work of the Swiss linguist Ferdinand de Saussure (1857–1913), successfully destroyed the realist myth of the literary text as a window on truth, encouraging instead a view of a text as a particular organization of language comprised of literary codes and conventions. Structuralism has been extremely influential in encouraging students to read texts as constructs, and asking them to recognize authorial choices and linguistic mechanisms as crucial elements in literary texts, but it has been criticized by poststructuralist, postcolonial, and feminist theorists for ignoring history and the particular social and cultural locations of texts and readers.

Poststructuralists share with structuralists an emphasis on textuality, but they deny that a system of interrelationships can produce a reliable system of signification. Jacques Derrida (1978) suggests that all words relate in an anarchic and unquantifiable way, so that meaning recedes further and further away from us the more we inquire into it. He shows how meaning is endlessly "deferred" and "differed"—two words he combines into "différence." Terry Eagleton (1983) explains that in poststructuralism, there is no possibility of a single founding reference:

> If you want to know the meaning (or signified) of a signifier (word), you can look it up in the dictionary; but all you will find will be yet more signifiers, whose signifieds you can in turn look up, and so on. The process we are discussing is not only in theory infinite, but somehow circular: signifiers keep transforming into signifieds and vice versa, and you will never arrive at a final signified which is not a signifier itself. If structuralism divided the sign from

the referent, post-structuralism goes a step further: it divides the signifier (word) from the signified (concept). (125)

Derrida's (1978) critique of Western metaphysics and of a fundamental Europeanization of world culture makes significant links with postcolonial literary theories. As Robert Young (1990) states:

> In its largest and perhaps most significant perspective, deconstruction involves not just a critique of the grounds of knowledge in general, but specifically of the ground of Occidental knowledge. The equation of knowledge with "what is Western thought, the thought whose destiny is to extend its domains while the boundaries of the West are drawn back" involves the very kind of assumption that Derrida is interrogating—and this is the reason for his constant emphasis on its being the knowledge of the West. (17–18)

Deconstruction involves the decentralization and decolonization of a European epistemology that is incapable of respecting the being and meaning of the other. It attempts to deconstruct the concept, the authority, and the assumed primacy of the West. Young also argues that, insofar as Derrida's notion of deconstruction involves a larger effort to decolonize forms of European thought, it can also be considered as characteristically postmodern: "Postmodernism seems to include the problematic of the place of Western culture in relation to non-Western cultures" (19). Seen from this perspective, poststructuralism and postmodernism have made significant contributions to the dissolution of the category "the West." Both have distinct political agendas that extend beyond merely deconstructing existing orthodoxies by moving into the realms of social and political action.

Linda Hutcheon (1995) agrees that the links between the postcolonial and the postmodern are strong and clear ones, but she points out that there are also major differences. Postcolonialism takes the imperialist subject as its object of critique, while postmodernism critiques the subject of humanism. From a literary perspective, postcolonialism and postmodernism often place textual gaps in the forefront, but, as Hutcheon points out, "their sites of production differ," with postcolonialism addressing gaps produced by the colonial encounter and poststructuralism considering gaps produced by the system of writing itself (131).

Poststructuralism, like postmodernism, emphasizes the constructedness of literary texts, and identifies the processes of ideological concealment in literature. Through deconstruction, readers can see how texts are complex constructs rather than transparent vessels of universal truths. In this view, a text is what Roland Barthes (1978) calls a "multi-dimensional space," open to a multiplicity of meanings, portraying the world's plurality and incoherence. Barthes's views on texts as playful constructs complement Bakhtin's notions of heteroglossia and have created possibilities for readers to engage in new forms of literary criticism and response. As Nicolas Tredell (1987) describes, the work of Barthes and Derrida has successfully raised new questions for students and teachers reading literary texts:

> Their ontological and epistemological challenges have raised important issues for critical theory and practice—for instance: what is an "author," a "reader," a "text?" How do we "know" the text? Does the text "know" us? How does "text" relate to "world?" They have helped to contest the tyranny of interpretations fixed to an appeal to authority rather than by argument....They have widened our sense of the possibilities of meanings in texts. They have drawn attention to texts previously ignored, neglected, or deprecated in the drive to discover a univocal message, an organic unity. They have enabled us to see classic texts in different ways...and to approach "difficult" twentieth-century texts...with potentially more rewarding reading strategies. (102)

Poststructuralist theories invite readers to see widening possibilities for textual interpretation, to value plurality and ambiguity rather than to seek only for a univocal unity of meaning. As Thomson (1992) indicates, such theories help teachers to "develop the kinds of strategies of resistance to beguiling and persuasive texts that Derrida and Foucault point us to. We can teach our students to deconstruct texts, to read against the grain, to give neglected texts a hearing, and allow repressed voices to speak out" (20).

Poststructuralism and postcolonialism have both succeeded in moving readers away from regarding texts as ahistorical and unpoliticized. Both have a strong, shared concern with marginalization, with challenging hegemonic forces, and yet both have been critiqued by feminist theorists for their patriarchal underpinnings and their failure to acknowledge the "double colonization" of many women. Feminist critics have encouraged poststructuralist and postcolonial theorists to adopt a more complex and pluralistic stance toward Eurocentric (mis)interpretations of the other, and to consider poststructural reading strategies that acknowledge the heterogeneous and often self-contradictory identity of female subjects.

Himani Bannerji (1995) notes that although postcolonial writers taught her how to think about personal and political subjectivity under conditions of oppression, they omitted a fundamental component—that of gender: "My gender, race, and class are not separate persona or persons—they make and re-present all of me in and to the world that I live in. I am— *always and at once*—there all together, for whatever that is worth" (12).

Feminist literary critics join with poststructuralists in encouraging critics and teachers to revise assumptions about language, textuality, and canonization. From a pedagogical perspective, feminist critics have pointed to the domination of texts by men in school and college literature curricula, and to the portrayal of women in literature from a male perspective. Pam Gilbert (1983) argues that it is not enough simply to add token texts by female writers into school classrooms. She argues instead for introducing texts that have the potential to transform the realities of female experiences, for "writing that challenges male definitions of 'woman' and 'feminine.' Writing that refuses to rely on formulaic narratives, but speaks out instead with the authority of experience," and she advocates "classroom practice which sets up a dialectic between the truth literature suggests and the truths students' lives have taught them to see and accept" (29).

In addition, feminists of color have argued that many white feminists have ignored the intersections of race, class, and culture with issues of gender. Black feminists, in particular, have drawn analogies between the relationship of men and women and those of the imperial powers and their colonies. These critics challenge the politically and culturally partisan nature of the literary establishment and have moved feminist critics in new directions. As bell hooks (1994) elaborates:

> Significantly, as feminist movements progressed, black women and women of color who dared to challenge the universalization of the category "woman" created a revolution in feminist scholarship. Many white women who had previously resisted rethinking the ways feminist scholars talked about the status of women now responded to critiques and worked to create a critical climate where we could acknowledge differences in female status that were overdetermined by race and class. (124)

This enlarged feminist movement has encouraged the expansion of the canon of literature to include more texts by women and writers from previously marginalized cultural and racial groups and has helped teachers to consider the need to deconstruct not only the opposition male/female but all forms of social power, inequality, and domination.

Feminist criticism, like poststructuralism, strives to identify gaps and absences in a text. It encourages teachers to help students to look simultaneously at ways in which a text is constructed and also to value what readers bring to a text. The idea of reading as an active engagement between reader and text links with the work of Wolfgang Iser (1978), who has been in the forefront of reader-response criticism. His reception theory suggests a reciprocal relationship between reader and text; meanings are not inherent in either the reader or the text, but are produced by a process of interaction in which the text offers directions for a reader to follow:

Text and reader converge by way of a situation which depends on both for its
"realization." If the literary communication is to be successful, it must bring
with it all the components necessary for the construction of the situation, since
this has no existence outside the literary work. (68–69)

For Iser, reading is a pleasure only when it is active and creative. A reader
establishes interrelations between past and present readings, causing the
text to reveal its potential multiplicity of connections. Iser characterizes
reading as a kaleidoscope of perspectives, pre-intentions and recollections;
when the flow of expectations is interrupted, readers bring into play their
own faculties for establishing connections, and they fill in the gaps left by
the text itself.

Iser's perspective on reading encourages teachers to reconnect literature with students' lives through an emphasis on the imaginative re-creation
of the text and the social relevance of literary content. Literature is seen as a
series of experiences rather than a body of static knowledge, and reading
becomes the basis for increased understanding of oneself and one's world.
This perspective on literature may give teachers confidence to include new
texts in the canon of literature they presently teach, and to encourage students actively to question and reflect on texts they read. Jane Tompkins
(1980) points out that by legitimizing the inclusion of personal responses to
literature in the process of textual explication, critics such as Iser appear
willing to share their critical authority with less tutored readers. They have
invited readers to bring back all the idiosyncrasies, emotionality, subjectivity, and impressionism that the formalist critics sought to deny (224).

Louise Rosenblatt (1978) uses the term "transaction" to describe the literary experience. She reminds us that readers are individualistic in their
past histories as readers and that they differ in their strategies for making
sense of literature. Her view of reading brings into question the role of
teachers as authorized readers who are often unaware of the extent to which
their authority directs and subverts student inquiry. Patrick Dias (1992a)
points out that in a typical classroom setting, students are expected to have
ready-made answers to questions on the text they have been reading; there
is hardly any time allowed for students to reflect on their reading. A large
group format, he suggests, is inhospitable to deeply felt personal experiences with reading or to reflective and considered responses to literature.
Typical class settings promote the notion that students must move toward
consensus on central issues raised by set reading:

Students are not expected or encouraged to differ with each other or entertain
ambiguity. It is not expected that some issues will resolve themselves only over
time, will raise new questions, will emerge anew in other readings. It is ac-

cepted that tests and examinations demand definitive, final answers....If literary reading is truly an event in time, we must find ways of consistently demonstrating this belief in practice. (136)

Reader-response critics such as Iser and Rosenblatt have provided the
theoretical support for teachers to develop teaching strategies that are hospi-
table to individual ways of making sense of texts. The validation of personal response to literature may be of particular value to minority students
who are finally beginning to read literature in the classroom that enables
them to discover their own histories and to find their just place in society.
Teachers interested in developing a postcolonial pedagogy can encourage
students first to make these personal links with a literary work and then to
move to a more critical stance in which they deconstruct the ideological and
political assumptions of a text, begin to challenge the power structures embedded in the production of the text, and question how the text relates to the
social construction of their own lives.

Historically, there has been a move away from a humanistic belief in an
objective reality whose essences can be rendered transparently though language in a literary text, toward a more pluralistic view of reading in which
language has powers that writers cannot control, texts have multiple meanings, and readers engage actively and reflectively with texts to deconstruct
their processes of production, their ideologies and social contexts. Yet how
much has really changed in our high school classrooms in the early years of
the twenty-first century, or are we simply touring through the same texts
and perpetuating the same theoretical stances but with changing vocabulary? How different is today's classroom scenario from those days in the
1950s and 1960s when I uncritically read canonized literary texts in order to
understand universal "truths" and derive predetermined fixed textual meanings?

Gunnar Hansson (1992) contends that there is much inertia in the
school system, and that although changes in school teaching seem to follow
the lead of academic theoretical research, these changes take a long time to
be implemented:

It takes a long time—20, 30 or even 40 years—for a new approach in literary
research to find its way into school teaching and to gain a dominant position
there....Furthermore, it takes a very very long time to get an approach out of
the school once it has been introduced. (147)

One reason he suggests for this time lapse in schools is that teachers, once
they have completed their university education, can "lock the door of the
classroom and go on for another 30 or 40 years, transferring to ever new

generations of students the only approach they had been trained to use" (147).

How can teachers be encouraged to make a transition into a practice of postcolonial pedagogy, implementing strategies of poststructuralist, post-modern, and critical literary theories combined with a reader-response philosophy that also values students' personal and idiosyncratic responses to literary texts? Perhaps the increasing pressure of a rapidly expanding multi-cultural society that demands new ways of selecting texts, new ways of thinking about texts, and new ways of responding to texts will hasten changes in the classrooms of the future and encourage teachers to become what Giroux (1988) calls "transformative intellectuals," engaging students not only in the virtual worlds of literature but also in the production of critical knowledge in the classroom (90).

Travelers' Tales:
Teachers Testing Theories

Readers of critical fiction cannot approach work assuming that they already possess a language of access, or that the text will mirror realities they already know and understand. Much critical fiction dynamically seeks to deconstruct conventional ways of knowing. It effectively critically intervenes and challenges dominant/hegemonic narratives by compelling audiences to actually transform the way they read and think.

bell hooks (1991, 57)

[T]he boys started a list of food they wished would float past their window: muffins, porridge, kippers, scones, steak and kidney pie, potted meat, dumplings. Their father said if they ever tasted this insipid foreign stuff instead of merely reading about it in those blighted Blyton books, they would realize how amazing was their mother's curry-rice and khichri-saas and pumpkin buryani and dhansak. What they needed was an Indian Blyton, to fascinate them with their own reality.

Rohinton Mistry (2002, 112)

Many Canadian English language arts teachers would agree in an abstract way that they ought to be including works from non-Western cultures and from "minority" peoples into their English curricula, particularly in light of the changing demographics of their schools. Many would also be in favor of more pluralistic teaching strategies that might help to combat racism and prejudice against minority groups. In practice, however, they find this hard to do; in fact, some are hesitant about how to begin to institute these changes, particularly as their teaching lives are already fraught with increasing demands from administrators and parents. As Arthur Applebee's studies in the United States (1989, 1990) and Robert Cameron's (1989) study in Canada both found, English teachers have reservations about teaching literary texts with which they are personally unfamiliar and which have few teaching resources developed around them. Reed Way Dasenbrock (1992) argues that when teachers say, "I don't really feel that I have control over the text" or "I don't think I know enough about it to teach it," this is less a practical difficulty to be solved by curricular materials than a theoretical difficulty. He explains:

> To say "I don't know enough to teach this literature" is to reaffirm a model of interpretation in which the "proper" interpreter is the already informed interpreter. This is the model behind most forms of literary scholarship, but it takes on a particular form when dealing with cross-cultural communication. When dealing with texts situated in another culture, we feel that what is needed is someone knowledgeable about the cultural and historical contexts of the work. The proper interpreter of an African novel is therefore an expert about Africa, and in practice this usually leads to the conclusion that the proper interpreter of an African novel is an African. (36)

As Dasenbrock points out, this particular argument, in the context of postcolonial literatures, has been the subject of much bitter debate about whether "outsiders" are taking possession of texts just as Europeans once took possession of colonized countries. Taken to its inevitable conclusion, such an argument would discourage outside reading of any kind and indicate that the only culture one can study is one's own. This stance is an author-oriented one, suggesting that the position of authority in the reading process is the author and that the aim of the interpreter (and the teacher) is to try to approximate that of the writer.

Of course, trends in literary theory over the past decades have argued against such a stance, as the pendulum has swung away from a focus on the author toward a revaluing of the position of the reader. Reader-response theories in particular have argued against the supreme authority of the author in favor of a view of reading as a transaction between reader and text. Deconstruction, in turn, has made a different argument, pointing to the impossibility of capturing the author's intended meaning in a text that is always shifting and ambivalent. Dasenbrock (1992) suggests that for reading in a cross-cultural situation, we need to move away completely from metaphors of "possession" of a text toward a consideration of each reading experience as a new scene of learning (39). Such a stance means that we view each encounter with an unfamiliar work of art as a learning opportunity. In doing so, we have to allow that the author and the text will offer enough guidance to enable us to grow with each encounter. This learning, Dasenbrock maintains, "can take place on many levels, often simultaneously: the lexical, the syntactic, the formal or generic, the cultural, the religious" (42).

Dasenbrock's theories suggest that a teacher introducing postcolonial literature needs to move away from being the "expert" reader of a text with prepared answers for each anticipated question toward being a reading guide who leads the class through the experience of reading a text and is a co-learner in the reading process. This advice does not, I believe, mean that teachers need never consult a learning resource or never teach the same text twice, but rather that they should become more confident readers and teachers of literature from unfamiliar cultures, knowing that there will always be aspects of the text that will remain unfamiliar. Whenever we read a new literary work, we have to trust that the words on the page will offer us at least a partial understanding of a new world. As Dasenbrock (1992) suggests, "All interpersonal communication involves translation and interpretation. We are never in complete command of the language produced by others, yet to live is to come to an understanding of others" (45).

Assuming that as an English teacher I accept the challenge of introducing my students to postcolonial texts, what dilemmas will I face? How will I even determine which texts to teach? Text selection rapidly becomes more complex when we move outside the accepted school canon. Of course, some teachers will have little autonomy over text selection, depending on their school situation. In Canada, provincial mandates vary, with most provinces offering teachers lists of "authorized" or "recommended" literary resources, with teachers having autonomy over individual selections, at the discretion of their particular school board and department. Assuming that I do have some autonomy to select and teach postcolonial texts, I might expect to face some of the following difficult questions:

- In a multicultural society, should I be trying to include the voices and experiences of all my students in the texts I select?
- Should I be concerned about the potential offensiveness of a particular postcolonial text?
- How do I balance the presentation of social and political values through a literary text with the literary merit of the work?
- Should I be concerned about presenting negative images of particular cultures?
- How much do my teaching and reading strategies influence my students' experiences with a text?

Peter Smagorinsky (1995) responds to a number of these questions from his own teaching experiences, suggesting, for example, that there is no way we can simply find texts to "represent" cultures in our classroom if we acknowledge that culture and identity are ambivalent, heterogeneous, and continually constructed and reconstructed through experience and through language. Smagorinsky concludes that "the goal of hearing multicultural voices in a truly representative way is impossible" (62). We need instead, he says, to help students to understand the complexity of people from particular cultures by introducing students to multifaceted aspects of cultural experiences in a variety of literary forms, including prose, poetry, drama, and film.

Smagorinsky (1995) also acknowledges that literary texts do not have the same transforming effect on all readers. People read in individual ways, bringing to a text their own experiences, backgrounds, and emotions. So, for example, some students reading *Huckleberry Finn* may appreciate Twain's dramatic irony, recognizing how his characters reveal the folly of a racist society, while other readers may be too humiliated or angry at Twain's continual use of the word "nigger" to be able to move to a more detached reading of the text. These diverse responses challenge teachers who introduce such a text into the classroom hoping to promote mutual understanding in a pluralistic society. Smagorinsky explains that he has not solved his dilemma of whether or not to continue teaching problematic texts such as *Huckleberry Finn,* Wright's *Native Son,* or Alice Walker's *The Color Purple,* all of which, he believes, are exceptional works of literature but offer a negative and potentially destructive view of the experiences of African-Americans. We need, he cautions, to develop a great sensitivity in our teaching that reflects our recognition "that the experiences of some of our students may not enable a dispassionate reading, and at the same time we need to be very open-minded in listening to students' responses and trying to work constructively with them" (62).

Of course, the issue of which books to read is only a small part of canon reform. Moving to a critical pedagogy is demanding, involving in-depth considerations of the ways in which instructional contexts and classroom processes influence readers' construction of texts and of their own lives. A critical pedagogy must inevitably take into account that schools are political arenas. As Peter McLaren (1993/1992) reminds us, educators teach within a field of competing discourses and "classrooms are not simply the physical location where learning takes place; they are also the site of teachers' embodiment in theory/discourse and dispositions as theorists within a specific politics of location" (19). For McLaren, a critical multicultural pedagogy involves a collaborative discourse "in which thought and action combine to dismantle the structures that support oppression. In this way students can share in the critical transformation of both the self as social and the social as self" (12).

Similarly, Britzman et al. (1993) argue that multicultural teaching practices must include an effort to discuss race, class, and gender with attention to the demystifying of the old dualism of equity and difference. They warn that much of the current reform in multicultural education in the United States continues to be "Disneyfied" in an attempt to create social and class harmony. They caution that teachers need to move beyond a belief that "rationality leads to sensitivity." This logic encourages a naïve hope that students will unproblematically harvest meanings already planted in postcolonial literature. As Britzman et al. (1993) explain:

> Enlightenment attempts of this sort tend to locate social prejudices within the realm of the illusory or the mistaken and as problems of individual attitudes. The view is that by presenting students with the effects of racism and sexism…students would be capable of substituting the unsavory falsehoods that populate their own cultural maps (i.e. racism and sexism) with the healthy truth of an anti-sexist and anti-racist knowledge. Hopefully, this reasoning goes…the story would permit the hardworking student to "experience" the substance of what it means to be "woman" and "black"—to step into the shoes of "the other," to be "the other of the day"—and in this way to access some inner truth already residing in this experience. (197)

Beverley Naidoo (1992) suffered from some of the same naïve expectations in her British study in which she worked with a white teacher on introducing antiracist literary texts to middle-class white thirteen- and fourteen-year-old students. She found to her surprise that both the teacher and many of his students had difficulty in imagining and identifying with the psychological reality of oppression presented in the texts. When teaching Mildred Taylor's *Roll of Thunder, Hear My Cry* (1976), a powerful evocation of racism in the American South seen through the eyes of a young black girl, the teacher found it easier to identify with the white lawyer than with the black recipients of oppression. Naidoo (1992) explains that this was the first time the teacher had taught a literary work by a black writer and though he agreed willingly to take part in the study, he was increasingly uncomfortable with the experience:

> After an initially very positive response to the book, certain remarks he made later suggested a basic unease, for instance that it was "wordy" and, surprisingly that he thought Mildred Taylor must have been copying Harper Lee's *To Kill a Mockingbird* (1960) when writing because there were some similar incidents. He did not seem to recognise either the absurdity of implying that a black writer should need to copy from a white writer to describe black experience or that the experiences were not unique, but repeated thousands of times in the South. (76)

Naidoo explains that although a number of the students found the book appealing, only a few seemed able successfully to make the transition between imaginative identification with characters in the novel and the reality of "If I were black." Most of the students felt they had "learned more about 'other' people" and their frame of reference remained firmly fixed within a white vantage point. As one girl said, "From this book, I know more about blacks. I hardly knew anything about them before. I never knew that the whites treated the blacks like that." Another student commented, "This book should be read in all schools because it teaches about how the blacks were persecuted and a lot of people are in the dark and it's important they should know what the blacks went through at this time" (77). There was little evidence that reading the book had disturbed the emotions of either of these students or had moved them toward an interrogation of the structures of power in society. Other students, Naidoo speculates, may have had their racist frames of reference more deeply entrenched by reading Taylor's novel. For instance, one boy explained after he had completed Taylor's book, "I knew most of what they were telling me. The blacks are a subject which we regularly hear about and are common knowledge." Naidoo wonders whether for this boy "the net result of reading *Roll of Thunder, Hear My Cry* was not simply to produce a better-informed racist?" (80).

African-American literature was also the focus of a study in the United States (Spears-Bunton 1990) in an eleventh-grade honors English class of "poor and working-class African-American and European-American students" with a "history of racially motivated animosity" (566). Paula, the experienced white teacher in this study, was disenchanted with students' responses to the canonized literature she had previously taught, and she was eager to respond to her students' requests for more African-American texts. Despite having completed a master's degree in English, she confessed to having little previous familiarity with this literature. At first, she continued with her formal style of teaching, which included units on grammar and vocabulary, and she used African-American slave narrative texts to supplement her traditional literature teaching of *The Scarlet Letter*. She discovered that the racial tensions in the class actually increased during the teaching of these texts, with many of her African-American students ridiculing Hawthorne's novel, or refusing to read it, and her European students generally being silent during the reading of the slave narratives or, in a few cases, claiming to "hate Black literature" (570).

Feeling somewhat desperate, Paula offered her students a different novel, Virginia Hamilton's *The House of Dies Drear,* and allowed class time for reading. Instead of continuing with her usual routine of teaching, she allowed students time to question the text, to engage in group discussions and interpretations, and to write more informally about the novel. This time far more students became engrossed in the literature, and during personal interviews, a number of both African-American and European-

American students acknowledged that they had engaged with this book personally and affectively and some claimed they had started to question their old assumptions about racial identity and discrimination. Spears-Bunton (1990) summarizes her reflections on this study:

> On an individual level the reading of culturally conscious texts may provide a bridge upon which both African American and European American adolescent readers may build and ultimately expand their literary experiences....Paula's introduction of African American literature into her curriculum invited individual and group confrontation on difficult issues of race, sex and class; yet, importantly, students crossed perceptual, gender and cultural lines as they engaged the world of the text. (573–74)

Spears-Bunton's discussion of the study, although it offers few particulars about aspects of the teaching process and about individual students' responses to reading the African-American texts, does reinforce the crucial role of teaching strategies in the introduction of postcolonial literature. It reinforces Dasenbrock's point that teachers need to move away from considering themselves as the "expert" on the texts they teach, allowing themselves and their students to approach multicultural texts as new learning experiences, engaging in an active dialogue with the words of the page and with other readers of the text. The teacher in this study was more committed to the teaching of the postcolonial texts than the teacher in Naidoo's study and more aware of the conflicting responses of her students. She learned that, although attention to text selection is crucial, reading multicultural texts in isolation will not immediately change students' consciousness, and she found that reading practices are inextricably linked with culture, politics, and society. As Ashcroft, Griffiths, and Tiffin (1989) claim, "postcolonialism...is best conceived as reading practice" (193). The study of postcolonial literature, they explain, is essentially political in that its development and the theories that accompany this development "radically question the apparent axioms upon which the whole discipline of English has been raised" (195). No study of this literature can pretend to occlude the specific national, cultural, and political grounding of the texts being studied.

Wolff (1996), attempting to engage her first-year university students in a critical pedagogy, set out specifically "to make antiracist pedagogies central to the task of educating students to enliven a wider and more critically engaged public culture" and to encourage her students "not merely to take risks but also to push against the boundaries of an oppressive social order" (324). Wolff describes how she combines critical pedagogy with Mary Louise Pratt's contact-zone theory, a metaphor for the "imaginary spaces where differing cultures meet" (316). Quoting Pratt (1991), she explains that this "contact zone" refers to "social spaces where cultures meet, clash, grapple with each other, often in contexts of highly asymmetrical relations of power, such as colonialism, slavery, or their aftermaths as they are lived out in the world today" (318). Wolff describes her attempt to introduce this contact-zone theory to students through the teaching of Toni Morrison's novel *Beloved,* considering ways Morrison brings orality and literacy together as Sethe begins to "rememory" her experiences of slavery in an oral narrative that subverts Schoolteacher's attempts to inscribe Sethe's experience into his own written text.

Reflecting on her experiences with one particular class of students, Wolff admits the difficulties of practicing a postcolonial pedagogy. She found that although a few students willingly took part in the critical dialogue of the contact zone, most insisted on a resistant reading of the text on their own terms.

> To be very honest, most were resistant to the reading, as was evident in many of their reading journals. Most could not abide the nonlinearity of the book.... Many wanted me to supply a plot summary; many, I suspect, wished for Cliffs Notes to accompany their reading. A few said that they stuck with the book, read as if they knew what was going on, powered through, and were rewarded at around midpoint with meaning. Fragments were beginning to add up for them. It was with and through that fragmented reading experience—a reading that made demands on the students, a reading that disrupted their conventional notions about narrative patterns—that students began to see not only what was privileged in the 1850s slave culture but also what sort of reading is privileged in the academy....The subverted narrative of *Beloved* confounded the conventional, orderly presentation of material to be learned, what the students had come to expect from the classroom environment. (322–23)

Using the idea of this subverted narrative, Wolff attempted to create a "safe space" in her classroom for students to construct meaning from the text for themselves through journals, small-group talk, and initiatory writing. She hoped they would come to understand how print culture is privileged and colonizes those who cannot read and come to see how *Beloved* exposes cultural and institutional boundaries that support racism. She believed that identifying those boundaries in the novel would allow students to confront their own racist positions. "The idea of the contact zone, the reading about historical context zones, and becoming part of a contact zone in the 'safe house of the classroom'" was intended to allow students to link schooling with real life and to a broader notion of cultural politics (324). Many of her students resisted such ideas, critiquing instead Wolff's selection of the text and her strategies of classifying print and oral cultures in her own terms. Instead of feeling she was practicing a critical pedagogy, Wolff ended up feeling she was centering herself and relegating her students to the borders of knowledge. She watched as her idea of using the metaphor of the contact zone as a screen through which to read a complex novel changed. Instead, it become an active metaphor in the classroom, with herself as the oppressive social order that students pushed against. She advises: "Students know marginalization when they see it, and perhaps not even classrooms that want to be 'safe houses' can be very safe, either for students or for teachers" (326).

Wolff's experiences highlight the complexities of practicing a critical postcolonial pedagogy. Students and teachers enter the classroom with their own prejudices, their personal, cultural, political, and reading histories and their inevitably idiosyncratic responses to literary texts. This is not to suggest that a postcolonial pedagogy should not be attempted, but rather that teachers should not expect all students willingly to participate in fulfilling a particular pedagogical, political, and critical agenda. Wolff believes that her experiences have helped her to understand that perhaps the best that teachers can do is to read theory and then problematize it, recognizing that no theory will slide effortlessly into practice or be introduced without resistance from some students.

In James Greenlaw's (1994) Canadian study, in which he set out to initiate a postcolonial pedagogy, he worked with a variety of students across Canada as they read and responded to postcolonial texts. In one part of the study, a class of grade 10 students in Vancouver, 40 percent of whom were Chinese-Canadians, discussed Asian-Canadian short stories with bilingual students in an international high school in Japan through an Internet connection; another class of grade 12 students corresponded via e-mail with Native students on a reserve, and a third class of Ontario grade 13 students worked on independent projects, comparing and contrasting racist representations in various films and literary texts. Using what he terms "postcolonial deconstructions of literary representations of place," (36) Greenlaw hoped students would "learn how to avoid thinking about people and their worlds in stereotypical terms" and to understand that "we can only *know* a place from our biased perspectives" (37). Greenlaw's study indicates that for the growing number of Canadian students with bicultural identities who have access to new communication technology, "there is no such thing as a pure cultural insider" (226) and that all students who are reading across cultures can easily circumvent stereotypes of people according to their cultural backgrounds.

In their Internet discussions of the short story "Spring Storm" by contemporary Japanese writer Mori Yoko, students in Canada and in Japan considered questions of gender equity raised in the story, examined the stereotypes of male/female relationships that Mori Yoko constructs in her fiction, shared their interpretations of the story's themes, and questioned elements of the story's translation from Japanese into English. Greenlaw (1994) concluded that

> students' reading of "Spring Storm" very effectively identified the multiple and conflicting discourses both within the story and within Japanese society. It is not at all clear, however, that the same could be said of a traditional reader-response approach had we simply asked the students in Vancouver to discuss their views about the story with their classmates instead of sharing them with their Kyoto key pals. (246)

Similarly, Greenlaw's Native students in British Columbia, in computer discussions about family relationships and racism with non-Native students in Ontario, were able to consider similarities and differences in the ways that their different communities had been affected by institutionalized racism. His grade 13 students, who were not involved in on-line conversations, compared and contrasted cultural and racial representations in various texts. One student compared representations of "blackness" and "whiteness" in the novel *A Dry White Season* by white South African writer André Brink and in Spike Lee's American film *Do the Right Thing*. A second student compared representations of black men in Hemingway's *Green Hills of Africa* with those in Achebe's *No Longer at Ease,* and another compared representations of Indian women in Forster's novel *A Passage to India* with those in Mukherjee's novel *Jasmine* and in her short story "The Management of Grief." Greenlaw believes that the comparative analysis these students attempted between the works of Eurocentric and postcolonial writers helped them to attain a sophistication in their understanding "of the differences between the writing, for example, of the tourist, Ernest Hemingway, and the resistance writer, Chinua Achebe, which they could not have achieved without border pedagogy's postcolonial approach to the development of multicultural literacy" (289).

Greenlaw's study is important because it offers insight into the potential for Canadian teachers to initiate a postcolonial pedagogy both within the confines of a traditional classroom format and through the use of technology. It points to the need to expand multicultural literacy into the area of multimedia, to consider using hypertext computer software to enhance multicultural intertextuality, and to tap into largely unexplored areas of Internet potential whereby students could become virtual travelers as they engaged in cross-cultural literary communication with students across the world.

With the experiences of these "travelers' tales" in the foreground, my journey is approaching the site of my own research, working with an experienced Canadian English teacher as she attempts to bring her own theories of a postcolonial literary pedagogy to the practice of her teaching.

Traveling Companions:
Research Revelations

The boundaries of identity and difference are continually repositioned in rela-
tion to varying points of reference. The meanings of here and there, home and
abroad, third and first, margin and centre keep on being displaced according
to how one positions oneself.

Trinh T. Minh-ha (1994, 20)

To experiment with a radical pedagogy is a minor risk compared with what the
inheritors of the colonial legacy everywhere in the world are obliged to live
with.

Ato Quayson (2000, 184)

More than twenty years after I left South Africa, I met Meg, an experienced
high school English teacher on study leave at the university from a multiethnic high school. We discovered that we shared common interests in
reading postcolonial literature and were both excited at the possibilities for
teaching some of this literature in school. Meg felt that although her student
population had become far more culturally diverse during the preceding
decade, there was little recognition of this diversity in the literature being
taught at her school. During Meg's year of study she focused her reading
interests on Asian and Asian-Canadian literatures and took a number of
courses for her master's degree in the area of Second Language learners.
We discussed possibilities for a collaborative research project at her school
during the following year when she would be back teaching.

The school where Meg had taught for several years had a heterogeneous student population with a high proportion of students from Asian backgrounds, both immigrant and first-generation Canadians, as well as
immigrants from Africa, the Caribbean, and the Middle East. In addition,
there were Native Canadians and students from a variety of backgrounds,
including European. The school was situated in a predominantly lower

socio-economic area of the city, and though the administration and staff maintained a high standard of education and discipline, they had to contend on a daily basis with issues of poverty, drug abuse, and teenage pregnancy, and with violent or racially motivated incidents. A number of students lived in situations of poverty or came from abusive homes, and although a proportion of students achieved outstanding academic success, many others struggled to complete their high school diploma.

At the time that Meg returned to her classroom, she had already been teaching English at the school for six years and she had gained an outstanding reputation with colleagues and students as a dedicated teacher. Outside her teaching hours, she volunteered her time offering lunchtime tutorials to help students who were experiencing language or learning difficulties or whose personal lives had interrupted their ability to focus on their studies.

Prior to beginning our collaborative study, Meg initiated her own study in a grade 12 classroom. She enthusiastically planned to expand her traditional canon of British and American teaching texts by introducing her final-year students to postcolonial literature. As the majority of her students of color were from Asian backgrounds, she decided to begin with Wayson Choy's "The Jade Peony," an eloquent short story about a Canadian immigrant family trying to cope with the expectations of two cultures. In lunchtime tutorials, many of her Asian students had spoken about the tensions they felt in trying to fit in with their new peer group and still meet their parents' traditional expectations. Meg hoped this story would offer a lens through which all her students could begin to understand these tensions.

Meg's optimistic expectations were quickly shattered. She explains:

> As I read the story out loud, I continually glanced around the room, paying particular attention to my Asian students. Instead of the slight nod or smile of agreement I expected to see, I noticed tension in their faces and hunched shoulders. Their body language spoke clearly but in direct contradiction to what I had anticipated. When I finished reading the story, the first comment came from one of my Jamaican students, "Boy, am I glad that wasn't about me." The impact of that statement quickly drained my misguided enthusiasm as I realized the pain of embarrassment my good intentions had brought. The story was beautifully crafted and spoke clearly of a common human condition, but my presentation of it destroyed any impact it might have had. I quickly reverted to the authorized anthology and a generic story that would not cause any further harm. (Personal interview one)

Meg's students, in ways reminiscent of Suzanne Scafe's experiences in a British university class, felt exposed and vulnerable with their traumatic cross-cultural experiences being made the focus of attention in class. Fortunately, this was not the end of the story. A week later, as a number of the Asian students came to Meg for extra help, they asked her where she had found "that story" and whether she had others they could read. When Meg offered to lend students her bulging file of poems and stories she had collected, they suggested instead that they would like to read them with her in their lunchtime tutorials. During the following weeks, Meg explained that she and her students "read one piece of literature after another and the students talked, laughed, and argued in response to the content of the poems and stories." When Meg suggested that they might like to evaluate the literature and make decisions about what should and should not be included as reading material in the mainstreamed academic classes, they enthusiastically agreed. In their subsequent sessions, students read, discussed, and negotiated texts to be included and texts to be rejected. Many of the stories that appealed to them emotionally were rejected because they were perceived as mirroring too closely "the truth about some of the perceived abusive practices in their homes," and students felt they "had enough to deal with in the form of covert racism without the added pressure to explain why certain unsupportive practices were acceptable to their culture."

Students rejected most translated stories by renowned nineteenth-century and early-twentieth-century Chinese writers such as Lu Hsan, claiming that the language appeared to be stilted in translation and that the characters' lives held little in common with their own lives. Similarly, literature that detailed the Cultural Revolution in China was rejected as unfamiliar, even though this revolution had caused many of the students' families to move to other Asian countries and eventually to Canada. One exception was the novel *Life and Death in Shanghai,* which interested two of the students, but which they agreed was "just too long" for general reading. Literature emerging from China since the downfall of the Gang of Four was axed because of the bureaucratic details of Communism, which students found confusing.

Students' rejection of a number of contemporary Chinese-American and Chinese-Canadian texts was more personal and complex. Much of the literature in newer anthologies such as *Many-Mouthed Birds: Contemporary Writing by Chinese Canadians* (Lee and Wong-Chu 1991) deals frankly with tensions created by conflicting cultures, concerns over cultural identity, family relations, language, and history. Students read these texts voraciously, but were hesitant about recommending them for general class reading. As Meg explains:

> Although my students never disputed the truths presented in the fictions, they did not want their Canadian peers to read about their frailties and their passions. There was a strongly articulated need to protect their privacy. They preferred

instead to allow the myth to be perpetrated that they were good, obedient students with no desire for active social lives. Many of the students were so concerned about their indiscretion in speaking about their personal lives when something resonated from the literature that they required continual assurance that none of the lunch-hour discussions would be communicated to their families. (Personal interview two)

The literary texts approved by Meg's students for class reading were predominantly contemporary works that questioned personal identity, wondered about "what will happen to me in this new culture?" and revealed depths of insight into the excitement, fear, and bewilderment of the immigrant experience. They included stories and poems by Asian-Canadian and Asian-American authors such as Amy Tan, Evelyn Lau, Garry Engkent, Jim Wong-Chu, Anne Jew, Grue Lee, Paul Chin Lee, Larissa Lai, Paul Yee, Denise Chong, Sky Lee, and Lydia Kwa. Students considered the chosen texts to be relevant to their lives without exposing customs or mores that might bring ridicule from their peers. They preferred stories written by Asian-Canadians and Asian-Americans to Asian stories in translation and to Asian immigration stories by European writers who, they suspected, stereotyped Asian cultures within a "national" culture and misrepresented their cultural traits.

Perhaps the actual texts selected were less important for Meg's students than having the opportunity to participate in the curriculum process and knowing that their opinions were being listened to and respected. Students spoke to Meg of the discrimination they encountered in school with remarks about their skin color, their slanted eyes, and their imperfect English. Many felt the need to be silent in classrooms because of their inadequate abilities in spoken English and the need to be equally silent at home about their feelings of frustration and anger at living in a country that seemed not to value them as worthwhile human beings. Meg decided that while she would make every effort to include her students' selections in future classes, it was less important to restrict her literature selections to only the titles selected by these students than to continue to offer students choices and to honor their responses to the literature being brought into the classroom.

This was the context in which I joined Meg to engage in a collaborative research project. We hoped to initiate a postcolonial pedagogy that would attempt to value the experiences of students from diverse cultures and simultaneously challenge all students to address issues of class, race, culture, and gender through reading and discussing postcolonial literature in the classroom. We agreed that I would help to select resources, act as a participant observer in Meg's classes, and interview student volunteers about their responses to the literature. We worked together initially on a pilot study with grade 12 students during one four-month semestered class, then continued the research in the following school year (September through June), with a different grade 12 class, a grade 11 Advanced Placement class, and two regular grade 10 classes.

Reflecting on my own perceptions of the practice of a postcolonial pedagogy at the time we first began the research, I understand now how naïve I was in my assumption that reading postcolonial texts could effortlessly "transform" students' consciousness and racial prejudices. Since leaving South Africa, I had read a range of postcolonial texts from Africa, Asia, the Caribbean, South America, and elsewhere, by writers such as Bessie Head, Chinua Achebe, Naguib Mahfouz, Jamaica Kincaid, Gabriel García Márquez, and Pablo Neruda, as well as the "hybridized" texts of such writers as Salman Rushdie, Toni Morrison, Maya Angelou, N. Scott Momaday, Michael Ondaatje, Neil Bissoondath, and Bharati Mukherjee. Feeling that I had done my students in South Africa such a disservice by introducing them only to Western and colonized texts that fortified a belief in their superiority to "others," I now believed that the introduction of eloquent postcolonial texts to student readers could allow silenced voices to be heard and racist hearts to be transformed.

Meg's assumptions and expectations were more pragmatic and cautious. With her recent unsettling experience of introducing the Chinese-Canadian story to her students, she understood a little more of the complex challenges of canon reform and student response. She was also embedded within a school structure that set its own constraints on text selection, text availability, evaluation, and teaching time, all of which served to temper my naïve enthusiasm.

As Meg prepared for a new semester of teaching following the winter break, I developed a "short list" of poetry, short stories, and essays available in a variety of anthologies of Canadian and world literature that I considered might be of interest to her grade 12 students. On reflection, I realize that I paid little attention to questions of text selection such as those raised by Smagorinsky (1995). I read eclectically, relying on available anthologies and asking advice from colleagues in Comparative Literature who offered their own personal favorites. I did not consider finding texts that might "represent" the various cultures in Meg's classroom, partly because it seemed an impossibility and partly because I had recently read Maxine Greene's article "The Passions of Pluralism" (1993), in which she cautions against seeing a person (or a character) as in some sense "representative" of a culture, thereby "presuming an objective reality, a homogenous and fixed presence called 'culture'" (16). As Greene advises, "We do not know the person in the front row of the classroom, or the one sharing the raft…by her/his cultural or ethnic affiliation" (16).

I looked for texts that seemed to have some "aesthetic merit" and that might resonate with adolescent experiences. Since I had limited experience in text selection, considerations of "good writing" drew me toward award-winning and internationally acclaimed authors. Because of classroom time constraints, Meg asked for short stories, poems and essays in preference to longer works. The list that I offered Meg (see appendices) was comprised of texts written predominantly in English, with a few in English translation, and I looked for a blend of non-Western writers and minority and/or immigrant writers in Western countries. I was particularly interested in including Canadian texts by writers whose voices had not been commonly heard in Canadian classrooms.

From my suggested list of texts, Meg chose five selections in two of the suggested anthologies and supplemented these with three other texts. She wanted to minimize the need to photocopy texts for her grade 12 class, and so decided to limit her selections to literature in two anthologies: *Literary Experiences Volume Two* (1990), an approved Alberta school resource that was already available in her school; and an American anthology, *Multicultural Experiences* (1993), developed for high school use, which she had already ordered for her school. Her selections included two Canadian texts (by Margaret Laurence and Carl Leggo); an essay by an Indian writer (Santha Rama Rau); a South African story (by Nadine Gordimer); two magic realism stories (by Colombian writer Gabriel García Márquez and Puerto Rican writer Rosario Ferré), and two Asian-American texts (by Diana Chang and Amy Tan) that had been suggested by her Asian students in the lunchtime tutorials (see appendices).

In retrospect, these changes to Meg's curriculum in her grade 12 class hardly seem revolutionary. I could argue that although most of these selections are by writers who share Rushdie's "hybridized identity," they could scarcely be described as a major break with a Western canonical tradition. The Canadian texts, for example, which Meg used as a starting place to begin to question issues of place, culture, race, and identity, are by mainstream writers, and the South African text, a powerful indictment of racism, is by a white writer. What I believe is more significant than the actual selection of texts is the major shift in intention that these changes signalled. Meg had moved from a previous sense of comfort and familiarity with her text selection and teaching to a new self-consciousness about the process of syllabus construction and an awareness of the need to move into new ways of teaching and responding to her students. Michael Apple (1993) considers that this heightened awareness enables teachers to understand the place of texts and teaching in the power structures of society:

> Do not think of curriculum as a "thing," as a syllabus or a course of study. Instead, think of it as a symbolic, material, and human environment that is ongoingly reconstructed. This process of design involves not only the technical, but the aesthetic, ethical, and political if it is to be fully responsive at both the social and personal levels. (144)

Looking back on Meg's initial efforts to reform her curriculum, I believe that she recognized a need for a new pedagogical commitment that involved more than just adding a text or two by a minority or non-Western writer. She was committed to advocacy for change in her classroom, and new text selection was an important part of the process. Meg had embarked on a journey of transformation that led her to interrogate the meaning of a literary education, and to question the process of making choices about the syllabus she was teaching. Such an interrogation enabled her to defamiliarize the conventions of teaching and to see her teaching through new eyes.

An examination of what it means to "profess" English and to teach it to students requires a reconsideration of classroom practice and a questioning of our political responsibilities as educators. We have become increasingly aware in the Western world how "Arnoldian suppositions" about culture have shaped our understanding of a literary education. As James Hall (1995) asks, "If we no longer aim to 'civilize' students by introducing them to a sense of 'high culture' through a literary education, what are our 'new goals' in teaching literature?" (7). Is it possible to offer students texts that somehow relate to their own individual backgrounds and hope that they will then share in the pleasures of reading? Does opening up the canon to new texts and new voices allow previously marginalized students to enter into the power structures from which they have been excluded? Meg's experiences with her Asian students would suggest that such good intentions are insufficient and may even be harmful in stereotyping students according to their cultural background.

Should we instead take on Gerald Graff's (1990) suggestion that we "teach the conflicts"? By juxtaposing various forms of literary education (high culture vs. low culture, mainstream vs. margin, etc.) and reading contrasting texts, can we initiate students into the history of literary education and engage them in dialogue about the academic and political debates that have shaped English studies? Would presenting literary studies as a dialectic in this way still allow for the hybridized, cross-cultural view of literary studies advocated by Salman Rushdie? Is the kind of dialogue advocated by

Graff possible in a classroom where some students are already compromised by social difference?

Perhaps teachers need to become "skilled readers of their own institutional locales and sensitive to the multiple needs of their students" and then improvise their own concept of how to "remake the canon" (J. Hall 1995, 9). It is this kind of improvisation that I believe Meg undertook as she began to teach her grade 12 students.

Meg was already aware of the dangers of attempting to universalize complex individual human experiences from listening to students in her lunchtime tutorials discussing their own hybrid traditions. She was sensitive to her students' needs and willing to offer them opportunities to make curricular decisions by including two of her Asian students' selected authors into her revised curriculum, and by asking her next class of students to vote on whether the literary selections she had just taught them should, or should not, be included in the grade 12 syllabus for the forthcoming school year.

Although Meg claimed never to have perceived herself as the "expert" reader in the English classroom, she moved further toward being a "co-learner" in this new teaching situation where much of the literature was as new to her as to her students, and she had no background knowledge developed over the years as she had with many of her familiar much-taught texts. In introducing much of this literature into the classroom, she encountered the texts as a "scene of learning," rather than as a "demonstration of knowledge already in place" (Dasenbrock 1992, 39). Such a position is not without discomfort for both teacher and students. At times, Meg wished for more background knowledge about a writer of a text, for a historical grounding of a piece of literature, or for an in-depth understanding of the particular literary tradition out of which a text arose. Occasionally she struggled with unfamiliar metaphors and linguistic connotations. A number of her students were frustrated by a lack of definite answers on meanings in a text, either choosing to believe that Meg did not wish to share her "expert" insight, or feeling uncomfortable with ambiguity. In one instance, a student asked Meg after class why she had chosen to teach a text she "didn't understand properly" herself.

Accepting ambiguity is, of course, a feature of both reader response and poststructuralist criticism. Iser (1978) defines a text as a blueprint with potential meanings to be activated by a reader, and poststructuralism considers a text to be a dynamic entity with no fixed meanings. As Dias (1992a) notes, "Literary texts afford possibilities of meaning rather than merely concealing meanings that can only be realized by close analysis" (133). These perspectives require teaching strategies that enable readers to work from their own responses and yet remain open to further possibilities of interpretation. Meg already had developed teaching strategies that supported this dynamic view of reading, encouraging dialogue and allowing her students to negotiate literary understandings in small-group talk, in informal writing, in drama activities, and in supportive large-group discussions. Expanding her class texts to include more unfamiliar literature reinforced the value of students and teacher negotiating meanings together.

The revision of a unit of literature in one English classroom in our pilot study seems a minor achievement, particularly bearing in mind that the grade 12 unit was only one part of a course that also included a Shakespearean play, a modern play, and book talks by students on self-selected fiction and nonfiction titles from a prepared list. The change was crucial, however, in setting a context for our further research. These grade 12 students' out-of-class discussions about a number of the texts encouraged Meg's next class of grade 11 students to ask if they could read some of the same kind of literature the following year; other teachers on staff began to take an interest in the new texts and were considering using Applebee and Langer's (1993) anthology for their own teaching, and, perhaps most importantly, Meg felt encouraged in her endeavors to extend the research into other grade levels.

For Meg, this was the start of a new kind of postcolonial teaching which opened up possibilities for hearing students' voices, allowed them entry into the "multidimensional facets of life, culture and knowledge" (Johnston 1994), and introduced them to the political and ideological assumptions of text production, text selection, and literary reading. This pedagogy included examining the assumptions and practices of the dominant Western culture and learning ways to read and discuss literature that promoted critical reflection and an increasing sociocultural awareness.

In attempting to "map" Meg's teaching experiences with a variety of grades, I have selected three different lenses through which I re-present the research data. Accepting the impossibility of creating any kind of mimetic representation of these research sites that would offer readers a transparent reflection of Meg's teaching and of her students' engagement with multicultural texts, I attempt to represent the study in a variety of formats that focus on both extratextual and intertextual aspects of the research. At mile nine, responses to the multicultural texts from grade 12 students in both the pilot study and the subsequent grade 12 class who volunteered to be interviewed are juxtaposed with excerpts from the literary texts in a dialogic format. At mile ten, I offer a close-up view of the grade 10 class in which I spent two terms as a participant observer, re-created through "photo/graphs" comprised of research journal entries, excerpts from students' writing, and oral responses. At mile eleven, I attempt to move into what Homi Bhabha describes as a "Third Space," re-creating the tensions evoked in grade 11 students' engagement with a literary text that interrogated their constructions of personal identity. In juxtaposing selected elements from my data with literary text fragments, theoretical ideas, and personal reflections in three different formats, I attempt to convey "re-presentation" as an active process of creation rather than a passive mirroring of a research situation.

Voices En Route:
Students and Texts in Dialogue

Language is the landmass that is constantly under our feet and the feet of others and allows us to get to each other's places. We bring the words, set in the intensely suggestive sequences and cadences of the writer, into ourselves. We engulf them in our consciousness and allow ourselves to be affected by them.

Sven Birkerts (1994, 204)

Dialogic relationships are a much broader phenomenon than mere rejoinders in a dialogue laid out compositionally in the text; they are an almost universal phenomenon, permeating all human speech and all relationships and manifestations of human life—in general, everything that has meaning and significance.

Mikhail Bakhtin (1984, 40)

As Meg and I initiated our collaborative research with her grade 12 students, we selected texts that had a predominantly cross-cultural focus. We began with two Canadian texts: Carl Leggo's poem on his native Newfoundland, and Margaret Laurence's essay "Where the World Began," in which she eloquently ponders the significance of the place where she grew up in forming her views of the world. Then we introduced students to Santha Rama Rau's nostalgic reflections on her native India. We wanted students to begin to consider the significance of their cultural and historical pasts in helping to shape their lives, and from there to look outwards and to see ambivalences in their own cultural heritages and intersections between their own lives and those of others.

We chose texts in a variety of genres and introduced students to various writing styles and techniques. All the selected literature, in some way, imaginatively addresses issues of culture and identity. Some of the texts, including Amy Tan's story "Two Kinds" and her essay "Mother Tongue," speak directly to immigrant experiences, diasporic identities, and questions of language. Others, such as Nadine Gordimer's ironic story "Happy Event" and Gabriel García Márquez's fable "A Very Old Man with Enormous Wings," offer subtle critiques of racism and experiences of exclusion.

Students found some of the texts more accessible than others. Nadine Gordimer's use of irony confounded several students at first reading. Most students were unfamiliar with magic realist literature and were initially perplexed when reading the Márquez and Ferré stories. In particular, Rosario Ferré's story "The Youngest Doll" presented these grade 12 students with a number of challenges with its enigmatic and metaphoric style and ambiguous ending. Meg was aware of students' discomfort and provided opportunities for them to read and discuss the texts in a variety of ways. She asked students to respond to the texts through whole-class and small-group discussions and through a number of writing activities, suggested in Applebee and Langer's (1993) anthology, which encourage a personal, creative, and critical response to the literature.

We understood from the start of the study that merely introducing students to these texts was insufficient if we hoped to engage them in a postcolonial pedagogy. Meg and I both had an interest in raising issues of race and class with students, in challenging them to see how these texts are embedded within conflicting and contradictory discourses linked to issues of power, and in unsettling students' complacency with respect to Eurocentrism. We were also both concerned with issues of gender and looked for texts such as "The Youngest Doll," in which the writer raises feminist concerns and questions.

For some students in these classes, reading the literature evoked memories and experiences of the past, raised previously unarticulated questions, and challenged them to think more deeply about issues of identity. For a number of students, their engagement with the words, characters, and narratives of these multicultural texts created the kind of dialogic relationships discussed by Bakhtin. A word, suggests Bakhtin (1984), is always an intersection of textual surfaces, a dialogue among several writings, a dynamic entity that links a writer, a text, and a reader in a particular cultural context at a particular moment in time.

In attempting to recreate the nature of such dialogic relationships, I have juxtaposed literary fragments with selected student responses in the hope that this format will animate the texts in question and recapture a little of the dynamism of the context in which the literature was read and discussed.

Simon:
I like English class better this year because it's a bit more open—it's hard to explain. The stories are more open and your writing is much more free.... I think the stories we've been reading are neat—you get to learn many different points of view from how other people see them.... "Where the World Began"—I liked that one, that was where the girl was talking about her neighborhood. We had to do an essay on that; that one was good—I like personal responses because you get to apply them to yourself; so it can help you to understand the story better.

Margaret Laurence. "Where the World Began." *Literary Experiences,* Vol. 2, 1990, 252.

A strange place it was, that place where the world began. Because that settlement and that land were my first and for many years my only real knowledge of the planet, in some profound way they remain my world, my way of viewing.

Carl Leggo. "Tangled." *Literary Experiences,* Vol. 2, 1990, 250.

far away
in a city you will never know
I chase words in the cold air....

Santha Rama Rau. "Return to India." *Literary Experiences,* Vol. 2, 1990, 338–40.

All around us, in Delhi, there were flowers. Yes, it is a tropical country, and yes, the climate makes this possible—but there was a personal pride and feminine joy in the country-women who tucked a marigold casually in their hair....I realized then that I had missed all of this in Russia.

Nina:
I'm Native and I've lived in Edmonton since I was two. I like reading stories that we can relate to—I like stories about life-styles—that show how racist societies are. I know that's true because I experience it every day of my life. I'm used to white people, as I live with them every day. But the rest of my family, they look more Native, they are darker and they meet prejudice every day when they go out. I hear stories of how they're treated—my mom comes home in a bad mood because a person won't talk to her. People stare at her or ignore her when she speaks. I like "Return to India"—she speaks up for her own country. Also that Margaret Laurence story was good—I see a need to defend your own territory.

Figure 1. Where the World Began

Sofia:
My parents are from China. I speak a little Chinese. That Amy Tan story was really good—it showed how Chinese families can have high expectations of you—expect you to behave in a certain way—it's hard for me to explain.... Times have changed now a little. Amy Tan's a little older than me—my parents don't force me to do anything I don't like, as long as I'm a good girl and do my home-work....It is the "American Dream" prompted the mother in the story—it's sad to see—all she wanted was a perfect daughter.... I'd like to read more Amy Tan—I hope it would make me more aware about China. I guess others should read about it too, but it isn't as interesting as it is for me.

Amy Tan. "Two Kinds" (from *The Joy Luck Club) Multicultural Perspectives,* 1993, 199.

My mother believed you could be anything you wanted to be in America. You could open a restaurant. You could work for the government and get good retirement. You could buy a house with almost no money down. You could become rich. You could become instantly famous.
"Of course, you can be prodigy, too," my mother told me when I was nine. "You can be best anything. What does Auntie Lindo know? Her daughter, she is only best tricky."

Rob:
My parents came to Canada from India. They had an arranged marriage. I've been to India once, but it was really boring there—not enough videos to play and the water kept getting cut off. I find English hard—I struggle with it. I liked some of the stories we read this year. "Two Kinds" is good. I can relate to it because I'm in the same situation—my parents want me to be an honors student and to be like an Indian student. I want to be me—I'm a Canadian. I had sympathy for the mother. She just wants the best for her daughter—she wants a good life for her.

Karen:
I like "Two Kinds"—it reminds me of me. I can understand others in class thinking the mother is a bag, but it's easier for me to understand her because I am who I am. I believe in different values from them, so I can understand the relationship between the mother and daughter—why she thinks like that. I like the story because it makes people know that they can think about the situation, about how others think about things. I find myself more attracted to stories that are related to conflicts like that of clashing of cultures—I like that because there are lots of little, little things besides "We just don't get along." Every time we read a story like that it opens my mind a little bit more and more.

Figure 2. The American Dream

Chris:
I'm not sure I have much to say about these two stories. I can't remember them all that well. Well, there was that one about the girl telling about her mother talking Chinese. It was all right. That "Two Kinds" one, that was about the mother and her daughter. It was just a story I read, you know, nothing I related to. It wasn't me or anything, it was just a good story to read. It didn't give me any insight or anything.

Jen:
I think Amy Tan's situation is like my situation. Two languages to learn and two cultural things. Sometimes it's hard to accept, like things I'm learning from school and things I'm learning from my parents, and sometimes it's like chaos for me. I don't get, like, the manners and stuff. Like, we have rules at our house that are different from the school and stuff. Sometimes it gets complicated...those stories really spoke to me.

Amy Tan. "Two Kinds" (from *The Joy Luck Club) Multicultural Perspectives,* 1993, 202.

"She bring home too many trophy," lamented Auntie Lindo that Sunday. *"All day she play chess. All day I have no time do nothing but dust off her winnings."* She threw a scolding look at Waverly, who pretended not to see her. *"You lucky you don't have this problem,"* said Auntie Lindo with a sigh to my mother.

And my mother squared her shoulders and bragged, "Our problem [is] worser than yours. If we ask Jing-mei wash dish, she hear nothing but music. It's like you can't stop this natural talent."

And right then, I was determined to put a stop to her foolish pride.

Melinda:
This year is more interesting than before—just, I guess, the stories that our teacher picks. Like, they relate to real life....Last year, we just sort of did old stories that showed you, instead of you having to figure it out on your own, what they mean. They're so real, the stories our teacher picked....I really liked some stories better than others— that story, "Two Kinds," the one where we could tell the difference between cultures, between our culture and their culture, and—you could see this on the Oriental people in class, the girls especially, you could see how they could relate to it. You don't realize what different cultures can do, how they relate until you read some of the stories that our teacher picked.

Figure 3. Speaking of Culture

Kien:

I was born in Vietnam, but my Dad came from China. We moved to Canada fifteen years ago.... Last year English didn't appeal to me. I just took it 'cause we have to, but, I don't know, this year I'm more interested I guess. Maybe it's the stories we read. That story of the girl and her mother—it sort of relates to how my lifestyle is. I think most Oriental people are like that. Like, they want their kids to get a good education and go to a post-secondary, preferably university and stuff, and, this relates to that story 'cause of how her mother always pressured her into doing things the way she wanted it. So it sort of relates to me, because I know right now my parents are trying to push me to go to postsecondary and try to get into university and stuff. I can say that story relates to my life.

Amy Tan. "Mother Tongue." *Countries of Invention: Contemporary World Writing*, 1993, 283.

... [I]t wasn't until 1985 that I finally began to write fiction. And at first I wrote using what I thought to be wittily crafted sentences...that... would prove I had mastery over... English....I later decided I should envision a reader for the stories I would write. And the reader I decided upon was my mother,...these were stories about mothers. So with this reader in mind—and in fact she did read my early drafts—I began to write stories using all my Englishes I grew up with.

Kwan:

I was born in Vietnam and we moved to Hong Kong and then to Canada when I was three. My English class is good—the stories are pretty interesting. I like the ones we're reading now—those Amy Tan ones 'cause they're interesting and apply to me too. That one story "Mother Tongue"—that applies to me because our language at home is different compared to language outside....I have to speak Chinese at home because my parents can't speak English that well—like, I used to go to Chinese school and go to English school, so that I was learning two languages at once, and I had trouble, like, getting good at both. So the story—it's kinda—yeah—relates to our family—like, I get embarrassed when my parents speak out and so does Amy Tan...and about being a child prodigy—when I grew up my Dad wanted me to do this, do that, to get good at some things, but I didn't like it, so, you know, I said, "Enough of this." It's exactly like what she did—she kind of rebelled.

Figure 4. All the Englishes I Grew Up With

Sofia:
"Happy Event" is my favorite story. That situation in South Africa, something like that could happen anywhere in the world right now. It shows you how some societies are. It reflects how minorities are treated sometimes. It provokes a lot of feelings in you as a reader. It gets to you emotionally. It makes you feel mad, angry, and very sad because you're so powerless in that kind of situation, except to try to be different in the way you are and how you react in a situation—to try to change your attitude.

Karen:
The story "Happy Event" I thought was so sad. How could one woman treat another woman with so little respect, even when they go through the same. One worked for her on hands and knees but the white woman stabbed her in the back—didn't even notice she was pregnant!

Nadine Gordimer.
"Happy Event." *Literary Experiences,* Vol. 2, 1993, 350, 358.

"The old house-cum-garden boy, Thomasi, began quarrelling with Lena, the native maid whom Ella had thought herself lucky to engage two months ago. Lena, a heavy, sullen, light-coloured Basuto, represented in her closed-in solemnity something that challenged irritation in [him]. Thomasi was a Basuto himself— Ella had the vague conviction that it was best to have servants who belonged to the same tribe, rather as she would have felt that it would be better to have two Siamese cats instead of one Siamese and one tabby....Ella looked at [Lena]...in a kind of fascination, and tried to fit with her the idea of the dead baby, rolled in a nightgown and thrust into a paraffin tin.

Nina:
"Happy Event" got me so mad to see that racism. I like stories that show this so people can realize that schools nowadays are not just one kind of people, not just white. That's so easy for me to relate to with being Native. I have so many friends that are different and they've had to face prejudice all their lives. I think we should read stories like this that have something to do with us. It's hard to get into one you have no feeling for. It's a good idea to read stories about something that can happen—happen in Canada—we don't realize it until it's shoved in our faces, so then we look again twice. Our English teacher treats us like real people who have opinions that matter. She doesn't just expect us to be there to learn from her.

Figure 5. Facing Prejudice

Melinda:

That story about the black girl in South Africa, I liked that best. I like reading stories about places I don't know much about because you learn more and it shows you the difference so that you can see it—instead of just growing up here and you don't see the surroundings around you or really notice anything until something happens and you have to notice. But when you read this story you can tell right away. You think what it would be like to live there and you can see how the people feel....My Godfather's black, but I really didn't think anything of it even when I read about wars and that on South Africa. I didn't think about how the people were, like, I heard about how they lived and everything, but, just through the news, so I didn't really think about it. But when this story came through, it really hit. Like, you could see how much pain they went through and what they had to fight for and all that. I felt sorry for that Lena, because she couldn't do what the white Ella did to get rid of the baby, but they did exactly the same thing and, boy, did they get different punishments. Ella went to Europe for six months and Lena had to work in jail for six months. Because there you really see the differences between white and black.

Kien:

That South African story, I don't know. I guess, yeah, I could say I enjoyed it, but I was just more amused 'cause, like, how white and black South Africans are treated 'cause like, before that, I was aware of the apartheid policy in South Africa between the whites and the blacks and how the whites dominated, but, like, I didn't know to that extent how the white people are, like, that much more dominant to the black people and how they're discriminated against. So, yeah, it's pretty interesting....I guess it's really important to read, like, from other parts of the world, because like, before, I didn't know much about it, so it's good that you read like, from other parts, not just from Canadian fiction and stuff like that.

Nadine Gordimer. "Happy Event *Literary Experiences,* Vol. 2, 1993, 361.

Lena got six months hard labour. Her sentence coincided with the time Ella and Allan spent in Europe, but though she was out of prison by the time they returned, she did not go back to work for them again.

Karen:

I couldn't speak English when we first came, everything was strange here at first. Now I can understand the culture....I like English class much better this year and I like the way our teacher teaches. I enjoy the stories we read, how they make me think and raise ideas in my mind. In class, I'm afraid to ask questions in a whole class setting—I love the small group discussions where we listen to others' point of view.

Figure 6. Unequal Justice

Chris:
It's that Márquez story—I liked that one the best. I read fantasy most of the time. And, you know, this one is based on racism and on discrimination, and I know I'm like that type of person who, well I don't like to say it, but I'm a little bit racist. I think it's just because of my parents. When I read stories like this, it changes some of my points of view, and I like that because it can just make me a better person.

Sofia:
Fantasy tries to represent what it is that happens in society today in a different sort of way. Yeah, that story did show how strangers who are different...how people can be cruel to them. I hope we're more educated now, and not as superstitious. They thought he was a freak, like the Elephant Man.

Gabriel García Márquez. "A Very Old Man with Enormous Wings." *Multicultural Perspectives*, 1993, 267.

...On the following day everyone knew that a flesh-and-blood angel was being held captive in [the] house....Pelayo watched him all afternoon from the kitchen, armed with his bailiff's club, and before going to bed he dragged him out of the mud and locked him up with the hens in the wire chicken coop....But when they went out into the courtyard with the first light of dawn, they found the whole neighborhood in front of the chicken coop having fun with the angel, without the slightest reverence, tossing him things to eat through the openings in the wire as if he weren't a supernatural creature but a circus animal.

Kien:
That "Very Old Man with Enormous Wings" was one of the stories I didn't really enjoy because I don't like that sort of story.

Jen:
I like fantasy and I liked that old man story, but I also think it's bad 'cause of how they controlled him. They kept that old man in a cage and they—they didn't give any respect to him. He gave—like, he brought them wealth and all that stuff and they didn't even think of that, they didn't even give him a decent home and a place where he could be comfortable. Yeah, it's bad, but it shows people how we should treat others—with respect.

Michael:
I like most of the literature this year. It's interesting, it makes you want to keep reading. I liked the old man story best. It's interesting how they showed how people can be prejudiced just because of the way that someone looks. It really relates to society today. People do judge by looks and you can't do that.

Figure 7. An Angel in Captivity

Carlos:

My parents came to Canada from South America and I recently spent a year in Chile with relatives. I speak fluent Spanish. I love Magic Realism and I've read some of Márquez's work before—I read *In a Time of Cholera* (*Love in the Time of Cholera*). I liked this Márquez story very much. It's so strong and shows us so much. We should read more stories like that, not just the same old authors. What our English teacher is doing is fun. She lets us see different points of view and to get a view of literature from other places. We just don't know about the writers at all. Everything we read— like the novel lists—there are hardly any foreign writers. Most are British and some Canadian. She's really my favorite teacher—she allows us lots of expression.

Gabriel García Márquez. "A Very Old Man with Enormous Wings" *Multicultural Perspectives,* 1993, 270.

...He seemed to be in so many places at the same time that they grew to think that he'd been duplicated, and was reproducing himself all through the house, and the... unhinged Elisenda shouted that it was awful living in that hell full of angels. He could scarcely eat, and his antiquarian eyes had also become so foggy that he went about bumping into posts...they thought he was going to die, and not even the wise neighbor woman had been able to tell them what to do with dead angels...

Shane:

That "Old Man with Enormous Wings" is a good story. I like the story. I got the point, I think all the stories that we've read are partly racism and about the way other people think, the way people deal with things, and that was a good story especially to get the point across. It does, like, depend on whether or not your mind is open to a race or not if it makes a difference. Because if you're prejudiced and you're reading say, Amy Tan's story, you would think that it was a stupid story. That would be their way to think, but I'm not prejudiced....So a story like Amy Tan's or this one could change points of view like, but it could also not, you know what I mean.

Kien: Fantasy doesn't appeal to me. It's just, I'm not really interested in that. I guess I just don't have an imagination. I'm not really creative or anything. I'm just more worried about the real world.

Figure 8. Seeing Different Points of View

Rosario Ferré. "The Youngest Doll." *Multicultural Perspectives,* 1993, 275–77.

...She had been very beautiful, but the prawn hidden under the long, gauzy folds of her skirt stripped her of all vanity. She locked herself up in her house, refusing to see any suitors. At first she devoted herself entirely to bringing up her sister's children, dragging her enormous leg around the house quite nimbly....As the girls grew up, the aunt devoted herself to making dolls for them to play with....On her wedding day, as she was about to leave the house, the youngest was surprised to find that the doll her aunt had given her as a wedding present was still warm....In the doll's half-open and slightly sad smile she recognized her full set of baby teeth....

The young doctor took her off to live in town, in a square house that made one think of a cement block. Each day he made her sit out on the balcony, so that passersby would be sure to see that he had married into high society. Motionless inside her cubicle of heat, the youngest began to suspect that it wasn't only her husband's silhouette that was made of paper, but his soul as well.

Karen:
"The Youngest Doll" was good—really spooky. I like the fantasy elements. It's like a little bit of a fantasy thriller. We can learn so much from reading a story like that—about how women were belittled then—and how time has not really changed that.

John:
That doll story was kind of stupid. It was too weird for me. I couldn't understand it.

Janet:
The stories we've read this term have been so interesting. "The Youngest Doll"—wasn't sure I liked it—it was really strange. I was angry to see how women were treated then. The whole class system forced them to be treated like objects. Because the aunt was upper class, she allowed the prawn to ruin her life. She was so embarrassed, and she thought she was useless. If she was lower class, it wouldn't have shamed her so much—they weren't expected to be perfect. We can relate that to our own society too. We have had to struggle to overcome that—we don't want women to be treated like that now. The themes behind the story really interested me. Even though it did bother me that it was so confusing, the story made me think and gave me real insight. It's one of those stories you keep on thinking about.

Figure 9. A Fantasy Thriller

Peter:
The story is so confusing. You read it and then you fantasize about it, like the story doesn't end when you stop reading it. That prawn was in the aunt's leg, but then it ended up in the doll's eye. It's like a freak nightmare show. It confused me but it made me think.

Su-Lin:
I'm still puzzled by the story. It was kind of weird. I haven't the foggiest idea what it means. Those two doctors—they were so evil....I found it interesting but confusing. It does give insight into women in society. When she talks about the sugar kings, she really makes us question status and power in society.

Rosario Ferré. "The Youngest Doll," *Multicultural Pespectives,* 1993, 278.

...There was only one thing missing from the doctor's otherwise perfect happiness. He noticed that although he was aging, the youngest still kept that same, firm, porcelained skin she had had when he would call on her at the big house on the plantation. One night he decided to go into her bedroom to watch as she slept. He noticed that her chest wasn't moving. He gently placed his stethoscope over her heart and heard a distant swish of water. Then the doll lifted her eyelids, and out of the empty sockets of her eyes came the frenzied antennae of all those prawns.

Carlos:
"The Youngest Doll" was interesting because of its portrayal of the status quo in that particular society—the structures of society and the role of women—and the way they were changing. It was very magical and interesting.

Laura:
I didn't like the fantasy story of the dolls. It was unrealistic and I didn't understand it even after we studied it.

Sofia:
I didn't find that story of the dolls very appealing but we had some good discussion on it. That's good. It's like last year when a lot of students they didn't bring up their concerns and they just stayed quiet.

Figure 10. Questioning Status and Power in Society

These student voices are diverse, idiosyncratic, questioning, striving to articulate responses to literary texts that arise from both personal and communal reflections on the literature presented in these grade 12 classes. Emerging, too, from this bricolage of texts and voices are students' efforts to explore their own ambivalent cross-cultural identities as they interact with aspects of the literature. The voices are also "selected" responses, shaped first by the original research context in which they were spoken, and shaped again in my re-presentation. Selected data, offered in this way, create their own particular story but inevitably fail to tell other potential stories. They can, at best, offer only a partial and fragmented view of the richness of these students' experiences. Like mythological travelers' tales, they create a fiction that attempts to evoke the aesthetic flavor of the original experience.

This echo of voices reflects back the nature of the classroom in which the texts were read, and implicitly re-creates the nature of Meg's teaching strategies. Students in these classes were not "told the meaning" of each literary work; many of them have created their own meanings (however fleeting) from the texts through independent reflections, small-group discussions, classroom conversations with Meg, and through personal and critical writing related to the literature. Some are still confused or dismissive about a number of the texts, while other readers are insightful and critical. All acknowledge the complex and often ambiguous nature of much of this literature. All have been affected in some way by reading the new texts offered in these classes and all have come to at least a partial understanding that reading postcolonial literary texts that reverberate with issues of race, class, and gender is a political endeavor with repercussions in the everyday world of living.

Students' comments reveal Meg's intent to raise issues of class, race, and gender in the reading of these texts. It is clear that Meg's classroom teaching involves a commitment to a Freirian perspective on literacy, a belief that when we read the word, we read the world, and a commitment to a classroom practice grounded in a belief that people's lives can be positively affected by critical reflection. As Jane Tompkins (1990) comments,

> What we do in the classroom is our politics. No matter what we may say about the Third World this or feminist that, our actions and our interactions with our students week in week out prove what we are for and what we are against in the long run. There is no substitute for practice. (660)

In the forthcoming mile of this journey, I offer a more in-depth perspective of Meg's teaching in a grade 10 classroom. Viewed through my researcher's lens, these close-up "photo/graphs" attempt to capture the day-to-day vicissitudes, frustrations, creativity, and surprises of a postcolonial pedagogy in action, re-created through comments in a research journal, notes on classroom observations, student writing, and individual student voices.

A Sense of Place:
Photo/graphs of a Grade 10 Class

All migrants leave their past behind, although some try to pack it into bundles and boxes—but on the journey something seeps out of the treasured mementoes and old photographs, until even their owners fail to recognize them....

Salman Rushdie (1984, 63)

The type of consciousness the photograph involves is indeed truly unprecedented, since it establishes not a consciousness of the being-there of the thing (which any copy could provoke) but an awareness of its having-been-there. What we have is a new space-time category: spatial immediacy and temporal anteriority, the photograph being an illogical conjunction between the here-now and the there-then.

Roland Barthes (1977, 49)

"The enchantment of art," Homi Bhabha (1996) writes, "lies in looking in a glass darkly—a wall, stone, screen, canvas, steel—that turns suddenly into the almost unbearable lightness of being" (205). With his mixed-media metaphor, Bhabha seeks to describe visual arts that lie between two registers of light: a mimetic light used to produce a visual image, and a quality of visible light used in contemporary art practice to denote an ironic reversal, a lightness that has its own specific gravity and is used to conceal and to camouflage. A narrative description of research practice may also be considered as a visual image, as a photo/graph, which attempts to create a likeness of the image of the research moment through articulating the "photo," while it simultaneously attempts to "graph" or decipher the image it creates. However much this visual image reveals of the research process, it simultaneously conceals and camouflages. In this "photo/graphic" view of my study with grade 10 students, the visual image creates a context for understanding the research, yet also subverts any notion of creating a mimetic likeness and emphasizes the impossibility of capturing a "true" picture of any research moment.

Although Meg taught two grade 10 classes during the year of the study, in my journal I limit my reflections to the experiences of students in one of these classes. This particular grade 10 class had twenty-five students, nineteen girls and six boys, mostly from European backgrounds. Students met three times a week during the school year for English classes. I was able to observe the class on average twice a week. Students exhibited a variety of academic abilities. Several students mentioned in my interviews with them that they had not done well in their junior high English language arts classes. A number of students spoke about how their parents struggled to make ends meet. A few girls in this class had left home and were living with boyfriends. One girl always arrived late for her eight o'clock class because she was responsible for feeding, dressing, and walking her two young siblings to school every day. Another had recently returned to school from living on the street. One gave up her baby for adoption during the first term at school; another was pregnant and frequently absent from class. For these students, their out-of-school lives often interfered with their ability to concentrate on their studies, yet most of them still expressed an interest in reading the literature and in being part of my research study.

In attempting to create a close-up view of the research, I have described the study through reflections in my research journal with excerpts inserted from students' writings and students' tape-recorded voices as they respond to the texts in individual interviews with me. (A list of the literature taught in this class appears in the appendices.)

Research Journal Entry: Wednesday, September 1

School is about to start and Meg and I have both been reading a variety of postcolonial short stories, essays, and poems that might be suitable for the grade 10 classes. Meg is making final decisions about which texts she will teach throughout the year. She is keen to address issues of racism and prejudice through discussions of the literature, and to try to help students make connections between the antiracist texts and their own lives. She plans to begin class by showing the South African film *Cry Freedom,* set in the 1970s, which depicts the murder of Steve Biko and dramatically re-enacts the escape of newspaper editor Donald Woods from South Africa after his banning. Meg has asked if I'll speak to the class about South Africa and help to set a context for Nadine Gordimer's short story "Country Lovers," which students will be reading later this month. She's also planning on teaching a number of anthologized short stories by Japanese, Thai, and Korean writers throughout the year and a variety of poems dealing with issues of immigration and racism.

Meg has also decided she needs to teach Harper Lee's novel *To Kill a Mockingbird* in the class because the school has a common grade 10 exam, so everyone in grade 10 has to read it! It's not a bad novel, but I think it really focuses on the experiences of a white middle-class family during segregation in the United States, and demonstrates their concerns about racism, while black experiences are merely the backdrop for the action and serve as shadowy figures in the background. Of course, *Cry Freedom* suffers from some of the same problems, as the focus of the film is mainly on Donald Woods as the white hero rather than Steve Biko as the black activist.

Meg had planned to introduce a novel by African-American writer Mildred Taylor as a companion piece to Harper Lee's novel in her grade 10 classes. She was unsure whether to select the first novel in the series, *Roll of Thunder, Hear My Cry,* or a later novel, *The Road to Memphis.* I'd originally suggested that she teach Taylor's *Roll of Thunder, Hear My Cry* for several reasons: The protagonist, Cassie Logan, is about the same age as Scout in Lee's novel; both books are set in the 1930s in the Southern states; and from a literary perspective the earlier novel is better written. However, when Meg broached this idea at a staff meeting, other teachers complained that *Roll of Thunder, Hear My Cry* is an elementary book and not suitable for high school. Meg then selected *The Road to Memphis;* this is the third book in the Logan series and although it's more plot-driven than Taylor's earlier book, it still stands alone quite well. Cassie is seventeen in this book and the novel is set in the early 1940s. We wanted to introduce it to students after they had read *To Kill a Mockingbird* in order to try Gerald Graff's idea of "teaching the conflicts." Meg ran into another obstacle with this novel too. Apparently, there isn't enough funding in the school budget to buy class sets of any new novel for grade 10.

We've now come up with an alternative plan. Meg is going to buy six or seven copies of four young-adult novels for each class and students can read these in small groups. With the help of the school librarian (who is very supportive of Meg's efforts), she's been able to slide the purchase of these smaller sets of novels through on the library budget.

I've suggested that we look for novels set in different cultures with adolescent or child narrators to link with Scout's perspective in *To Kill a Mockingbird.* Fortunately, we have some time to decide on our selections, as students won't be reading the novels until after the New Year. I've lent Meg some novels to read and to consider for the group study: *Harriet's Daughter* by Marlene Nourbese Philip (West Indian/Canadian); *A Hand Full of Stars* by Rafik Schami (Middle Eastern/German); *The Dark Child* by Camara Laye (West African/French); *My Name is Seepeetza* by Shirley Sterling (Native Canadian); *The House on Mango Street* by Sandra Cisneros (Mexican/American); *The Clay Marble* by Minfong Ho (Thai/Cambodian); *The Honorable Prison* by Lyll Becerra de Jenkins (Colombian/American); and, of course, Mildred Taylor's *The Road to Memphis*. The advantage of all these novels, although they are of varying complexity, is that the authors grew up in the cultures being described, even though most of them now live in the West.

Research Journal Entry: Monday, October 4

Classes have been underway for several weeks now. When I was in the grade 10 class last week, I spoke to students about life in South Africa, about Nelson Mandela and the first-ever democratic election in the country. I discovered that most students had little knowledge about South Africa at all. Many didn't realize it was even a separate country but thought it was simply the southern part of Africa. A few students asked questions about Donald Woods and Steve Biko, as they had recently seen the film *Cry Freedom*. Those students who did comment expressed their horror at the apartheid system and the apparent powerlessness of black people in the country.

Before viewing the film, students read Maya Angelou's poem "And Still I Rise." Meg hoped the poem would help students to understand how African-Americans have suffered from the same kind of racism and discrimination faced by black South Africans. Today in class, students read Gerry Weiner's speech, "Youth Our Best Hope to End Racial Discrimination," which he originally delivered in Ottawa to mark the International Day for the Elimination of Racism and Racial Discrimination, and which is now anthologized in the Issues Anthology entitled *Multiculturalism*. Meg hoped that reading this speech would help students to acknowledge that racism is a concern all over the world, including Canada. Students discussed the speech together, were asked to find pertinent words relating to discrimination in the text, and had to answer several questions about their own visions of Canada's future. As I watched students read and discuss the speech, I noticed few sparks of interest. Possibly the "dull" language of the text failed to inspire them. Unfortunately, Weiner's oratory eloquence is definitely not in the league of Martin Luther King's.

Research Journal Entry: Monday, October 25

For the past two weeks students have been reading and studying Nadine Gordimer's short story "Country Lovers," which is set in the South Africa of the 1970s and describes a friendship between Paulus, an Afrikaans white farm boy, and Thebedi, the young daughter of a black servant on the farm. Their relationship gradually develops into a secret love affair. Thebedi becomes pregnant and Paulus, fearing for his reputation, poisons the child and blames the death on Thebedi. At a subsequent trial, he is acquitted of blame. The story focuses on Paulus's inability to move out of the constraints of apartheid, and on the inner strength of Thebedi, as she accepts both the loss of her baby and the inequities of the social fabric of South Africa. Gordimer's understated yet eloquent writing style offers readers insight into the conflicting emotions of the protagonists.

When Meg introduced the story, she read it aloud, then provided time for silent reading. Students asked a number of general questions in a whole-class discussion, then, following a more in-depth discussion with Meg, they were asked to look at the story more closely in small groups, considering first their own responses to the story and then looking at themes, characterization, and writing style. Students were given class time to write out characteristics of the two main characters and were told that the story would become the basis of a writing project in which they could select their own title and develop their ideas about the story into a critical response essay. Meg spent time in class discussing the themes of the story and provided examples and a handout about ways to approach writing a formal essay.

The group discussions were generally animated, with students asking questions about the context of the story and making connections to their viewing of *Cry Freedom*. Most students were less enthusiastic about the essay. Last week, when they were to bring a first draft of their essay to class for peer editing, many students had "left their essays at home" and the peer editing was not particularly successful, despite the fact that Meg gave them guidelines for response. She has since offered students individual help with their essays, both during and after class, and all the essays have now been completed and handed in.

Research Journal Entry: Thursday, November 4

I've had some time to read and to reflect on students' written responses to "Country Lovers." The essays vary in quality, of course, with some students demonstrating an ability to deal more competently than others with the structural aspects of essay writing. In most of their essays, students have offered a plot summary with a discussion of the devastating effects of apartheid in South Africa. Meg's idea of asking students to select their own title has allowed them to focus their arguments on an aspect of the text that particularly interests them. Mostly, students are concerned with the personal pain caused by racism.

The following comments are excerpts from students' essays on "Country Lovers," with some minor spelling edits.

Tammy, who titled her essay "One Another's Pain," blames apartheid for creating an uncaring society. She writes:

> The theme of the story is expressed through the situation of two characters: Paulus, son of a white wealthy farmer, and Thebedi, a black servant working on the farm. These two are as different as night and day according to their society. However they commit a taboo of engaging in a secretive, interracial involvement…. The society that has been created in South Africa has only helped in hurting people and bringing on problems. Two people who cared deeply for one another can no longer be together because of this.

Andrea used the title "A Day in the Life of South Africans." In her conclusion she is able to relate to the situation in the story in a more personal way:

> Paulus and Thebedi were separated because of apartheid. Let's not let this happen to our children.

Brad used the title "Forbidden Couple." He is able to consider racism outside the South African context as he speculates on the couple's situation in other societies:

> Will racism ever die?…If Paulus and Thebedi lived in most of the other countries of the world they likely could have had a more open relationship and have more equal rights. This would be especially true for Canada, although there are still some people who are not in favor of blacks and whites having close relationships.

Susan called her essay "Apartheid in South Africa." She offers an insightful opinion that racism exists outside the legal system:

> Prejudice and racism happen frequently in our world today. "Country Lovers" concentrates on the issue of apartheid in South Africa….The law of apartheid in South Africa no longer exists. But that does not mean racism no longer exists. In the story interracial relationships were looked upon as disgusting, not beautiful or normal. The law of apartheid in South Africa succeeded in separating two loving people for life. The author made me realize how difficult life can be when it comes to races not being allowed to make their own decisions.

Jeff was more adventurous in using the title "Romeo Chickens Out." He moves outside the confines of Gordimer's story to relate the situation to Shakespeare's *Romeo and Juliet*. Despite the bantering tone of his writing,

Jeff is articulate in speculating on the impact of racism, and he clearly sees the power of story to evoke strong feelings about important issues of race and power:

> When you think about it, there is still a lot of racism in the world. In some places more than others. There is always some racial tension between races in different foreign countries that have been settled by foreigners. In our own country as well, it has quite an effect on people, some more than others. But I had no idea how much it can affect people or how it affects the lives of individuals. I had no idea, that is, until I read "Country Lovers" by Nadine Gordimer....
>
> At the beginning, the story seemed like an innocent story of two lovers, but when it ended, the romance is gone, and so is the love, and all we are left with is a cowardly Paulus and a brave Thebedi, who is ready to go on with life.
>
> If there was no such thing as apartheid in South Africa, would this couple have made it? I'll bet they would have. But as long as there is the kind of discrimination like that around, people will spit on the faces of couples like this. The fact that Paulus was a chicken didn't help much either. In fact, this story reminded me a lot of *Romeo and Juliet*, except Romeo wasn't willing to follow Juliet wherever she went and abandon her. But still, apartheid was still a major part in the splitting of these two, and if you ask me, this story does justice to the effects of apartheid more than anyone could say in a lecture.

A few students, such as John, are able to take a philosophical approach to racism, considering the difficulties of fighting against the norms of the society in which we live, and the need for courage to effect changes. John titled his essay "The Struggle against Racism":

> In the short story "Country Lovers" the main character Paulus lived in South Africa when racism and prejudice were commonplace. Paulus was not strong enough to control these forces....You are not born a racist or to be prejudiced. Just like riding a bike or doing algebra, you are taught this behavior. Paulus grew up in South Africa so being racist was almost expected of you by your elders. Like any young person, Paulus looked up to higher authority and believed in what they said. If you hear the same thing over and over again, naturally you will begin to believe in it.
>
> Racism and bigotry are caused by fear....This in turn causes them to be weak and hide behind the laws of apartheid. Paulus is so weak he even goes as far as killing his own child in fear of his father finding out about his relationship with Thebedi.
>
> Apartheid is now illegal in South Africa because of the great struggle by the black people and their great leaders such as Steve Biko. Without these laws people may now begin to realize it is better to be yourself than to be molded or shaped by some crazy fools of higher authority. People should be themselves and follow their dreams, not other people.

It is clear from students' writings and reflections that the story "Country Lovers" evoked the kind of empathetic outrage discussed by Maxine Greene and that a number of students were able to articulate their understandings of how unequal power relations create situations of discrimination and marginalization.

Research Journal Entry: Monday, November 22

I've been interviewing student volunteers about their responses to *Cry Freedom* and "Country Lovers." I was encouraged by the numbers of students who wanted to talk to me. Even when they had little to say about the texts, they seemed to value having an opportunity to be listened to. I've been reading Roland Barthes's (1982) book *Camera Lucida: Reflections on Photography* and I am reminded again that an interview situation is a moment in time; like a photograph it attempts to capture a particular person, a particular event in a particular context. Change the angle slightly, refocus the camera, and the image changes. Similarly, the responses of students being interviewed are affected by the research moment, by the particular context of their day and situation. Like a photographer, a researcher needs to be aware that the "subject" that is in focus is conscious of being scrutinized. The responses that students give are filtered through an awareness of the researcher's position and of the context in which the interview is taking place. As Barthes points out:

> Once I feel myself observed by the lens, everything changes; I constitute myself in the presence of "posing"...I lend myself to the social game. I pose. I know I am posing, I want you to know that I am posing. (10–11)

The most sensitive portrayal of a classroom encounter or a personal interview is still a kind of simulation. Although I believe we can learn a great deal from such simulations, we always have to acknowledge that they are in no way a transparent reflection of reality.

Most of the grade 10 students I interviewed commented primarily on the harsh realities and consequences of apartheid in both the film and the Gordimer story. Students who spoke about *Cry Freedom* expressed some degree of outrage at the effects of racism depicted in the film. Sharleen, for example, commented,

> *I liked the film, but when I saw the way the whites treated the blacks, I couldn't really believe it, because you know, you go around towns here and you don't see any of that. It's hard to believe in other parts of the world that's really going on.*

Sally told me: *"The film was pretty different. A lot of whites beating up the blacks. I've never seen that before. I haven't really seen how blacks get abused before. I've heard about it, but I never believed it really."* And Mary said, *"The film was pretty good. I didn't realize there was so much stuff that had been going on in South Africa."*

A few students made insightful comments on the racial situation in the film. Justin explained that *"Black South Africans may not have the power, but that doesn't give the white people the right to treat them like that. I think something should be done."* Another student, Mike, made a more direct link to racism in other parts of the world, comparing the situation Steve Biko faced in South Africa with that faced by Malcolm X in the United States: *"It was a good movie. It explained a lot, you know, about how it was before—for the blacks in South Africa. I thought it was like history. It reminded me of Malcolm X."*

In contrast, another student, Colin, seemed to have been totally unaffected by the film. He confessed, *"I fell asleep. I didn't enjoy it that much."* A number of students, although expressing more interest in the film than Colin did, appeared to have focused on the experiences of Donald Woods and his family as they escaped from South Africa. Joe, for example, commented briefly on Steve Biko's situation, explaining that he *"felt bad because of what the white people did to that one guy, how they tortured him,"* but he focused more on the story of Donald Woods, telling me that he *"particularly liked it in the end when the author got out. That was good."* Alan, another student, said, *"I liked the acting and the escape part,"* and Sharleen said, *"I hope they come out with a second part to it, like to continue on, what happened to all the family."*

I believe that these students' responses reflect the filmmakers' perspective in *Cry Freedom*. Even though they portray the harrowing experiences of black South Africans, they consider white people's experiences to be of more significance in South African politics. I am reminded of Toni Morrison's (1989) words, "We are the subjects of our own narratives, witnesses to and participants in our own experience" (9). Although the film *Cry Freedom* appears to have enabled students to gain more information about the horrors of racism, it did not seem to have the potential to raise students' awareness of their own involvement in the structures of power.

In contrast, most of the students in my interviews responded on a more personal level to Nadine Gordimer's story, commenting on the injustice of an apartheid system that forced the young lovers apart by making mixed marriages illegal and ensuring societal disapproval of interracial relationships. Generally, students seemed able to engage emotionally with the two protagonists of the story and to gain insight into the personal tragedies resulting from apartheid. Dawn, for example, told me, *"It was a good story. It shouldn't matter if you're a different color. You should just love each other. Thebedi was really nice and Paulus was just too scared about his image."* Mary also decided, *"It was a good story. I liked the black girl and the white boy getting together and then it made me mad because of what happened to her."* Anne commented, *"Apartheid is really bad because it stopped them loving each other, but if they were really in love, they could have made it somehow."* Even Colin, who fell asleep in *Cry Freedom,* conceded that *"The story was okay. It was better than the boring movie."* A few students, such as Andrea, were able to make a direct link between the text and their own lives:

> *It was very sad. It made me realize how I hate all the prejudice in the world. Because my dad's prejudiced and gets really mad. I hate it when he talks about all that, about "stupid niggers" and talk like that. I get really mad 'cause I'm not prejudiced and I don't see why anyone should be.*

Generally, the students I interviewed gave me the impression that Nadine Gordimer's story had resonated in some way with their own lives and had helped them to gain a more in-depth understanding of institutionalized racism.

Research Journal Entry: Friday, December 10

We are almost at the Christmas break. Students have been reading selections from a new school anthology entitled *The Storyteller: Short Stories from Around the World,* edited by James Barry and Joseph Griffin, which I purchased at a conference last year. Meg chose four Asian stories from the anthology for her grade 10 classes to read.

"Love Must Not Be Forgotten" by Zhang Jie is a Chinese story in translation about a young woman's decision whether or not to marry her "last-chance" suitor. Woven through the story are her mother's diary entries of her unrequited love for a man other than her husband. The story was not particularly successful in this class. Meg's efforts to read the story aloud revealed awkward phrasing and other linguistic concerns. We wonder whether this is a problem of translation or perhaps our own inadequacy at understanding the nuances of the story.

A second story, also in translation, "Swaddling Clothes," is by the renowned and controversial Japanese writer Yukio Mishima. This story juxtaposes a young woman's delicate and sensitive spirit with the crass materialism and class consciousness of her husband. The story has psychological depth and complex allusions to time and place. A number of students were confused by the narrative complexity, but the story had a strong emotional appeal and raised important questions of class and gender. Meg and I felt there were fewer concerns about the translation of this story.

Another story, "The Non-revolutionaries," is written by Yu-Wol Chong-Nyon, the pen name of a young Korean woman writer. The text is strongly grounded in a historical setting. The young narrator, returning to Seoul from study leave in the West, is engulfed in events early in the Korean civil war. She and her family are forced from their homes to watch and to applaud as fellow Koreans are denounced as traitors and shot. The author reflects on the injustices and cruelty of a war between one's own people.

Meg found that this story required readers to bring to the text some contextual understanding. In her other grade 10 class, she had introduced the story without offering students any contextual details. Most students appeared confused about the narrator's experiences. In this class, Meg began by asking students about the television show *M*A*S*H,* and then discussed current "hot spots" around the world where civil wars are still raging. One student, Jon, who had moved to Canada from Bosnia six years earlier, shared his view of the civil war there. Another student, Jenny, had been to visit relatives in Northern Ireland and spoke of her inability to understand the sectarian violence in that country. Meg then read "The Non-revolutionaries" aloud and students were able to make links between events in the story and the earlier class discussion. These experiences suggest that, although each student's reading experiences will inevitably remain individual, the specific context in which a class reading is introduced will influence how students read a text. In this particular case, Meg's discussion of civil wars, combined with individual students' shared experiences, created a meaningful context for the reading.

In contrast, "Who Needs It?," a translated story by the Thai writer Vilas Manivat, is an accessible story that seemed to engage most students on first reading without any background context being created. Using predominantly dialogue, this story describes an armed robbery of a storekeeper known for his generosity and kindness. The storekeeper's unusual response to the situation creates an unexpected human bond between the attacker and his intended victim. After reading this story, students engaged in lengthy discussions about ethical and moral dilemmas related to violence, and raised questions relevant to some of their own experiences.

In addition to the short stories read this term, Meg introduced a number of poems that focused on Canadian immigrant experiences, selected from the Issues Anthology *Multiculturalism:* "Our Subdivision" by Nigel Darbasie; "Equal Opportunity" by Jim Wong-Chu; "Heritage Day" by Bert Almon; and "Immigrants: The Second Generation" by Kevin Irie. Students responded to these poems in small group discussions, in drama and research activities, and through personal and critical writing. With each piece of literature, discussion revolved around political, social, and ethical questions. As Arun Mukherjee (1988) suggests, postcolonial literature can move readers beyond the predominant motifs of a modernist tradition to include themes of "conquest and subjugation, racism, sexism and class conflict" (4).

Research Journal Entry: Monday, February 14

Since returning from the Christmas break, students have been reading and studying *To Kill a Mockingbird*. Meg read large portions of Harper Lee's novel out loud in class. She chose exciting sections to read and was able to engage students in interesting discussions about racial discrimination in the context of the book and about point of view in literary texts. Many students obviously haven't read much of the novel by themselves, though, as they've struggled to respond to specific questions on the text, and some students are still confused about the characters.

Meg has made decisions about the four novels we'll offer students next week to read in small groups. Two were books I'd recommended as written from "within a culture"—Mildred Taylor's *The Road to Memphis,* an interesting parallel to Harper Lee's novel, written from an African-American viewpoint, and Lyll Becerra de Jenkins's *The Honorable Prison,* a fictionalized account of the author's adolescent experiences of being held under "house arrest" in her native Colombia. The two other novels, although also first-person narratives set in non-Western cultures, are written by authors outside the culture described: *Shabanu, Daughter of the Wind* is Suzanne Fisher Staples's award-winning American novel set in the Cholistan desert in Pakistan, and *Forbidden City* by Canadian writer William Bell is an exciting "day-by-day" fictionalized diary account of events leading up to the Tienanmen Square uprising in Beijing, as told by a seventeen-year-old Canadian boy visiting China with his father.

Students will be asked to make a first and second choice of novel to read based on our book talks, and we'll organize reading groups on that basis. We've made up a "time line" for the more reluctant readers to complete their book, although we'll encourage students to read the novel at their own pace and we hope they'll read ahead of the schedule. Meg has dedicated class time for small-group discussions, and organized a group project in which group members will prepare to give a book talk on one aspect of their selected novel, focusing either on plot, theme, character, setting, or writing style. Everyone will have an opportunity to hear about the three books they didn't read.

Research Journal Entry: Thursday, April 8

Reflecting on the small-group novel studies, I think they were a great success. Students in the class seemed very pleased to be offered a choice of novel to read. Of course, some of the appeal lay in doing something "different" from reading a class novel, and in seeing Meg arrange new sets of contemporary books in inviting piles on her desk. Meg and I prepared book talks on each novel and read short excerpts from each text to give students a flavor of the book and to try to make each novel appealing to adolescent readers. When we collected students' first and second choice papers, we were pleased to see that the selections were fairly evenly divided, so that only three students had to read their second choice of novel.

When I asked students in our personal interviews about the selection process, they were unanimous in applauding the idea of self-selecting texts, even though the options were limited. Fanny, for example, said, *"I liked that. Usually we don't have any options. We just read this and then do that. But this time we had a choice, so I chose* The Road to Memphis.*"* Mike commented, *"Yeah, that's good. You get a choice of what you want to read instead of like, having to do a book. If you're not interested in it, you're not going to like the book."* Lynn reinforced the same idea, saying, *"A lot of times the books I have to read I don't want to, and this way I got to choose something that I knew I would read."*

For students such as Jared and June, who told me they did not enjoy reading, being given the opportunity to participate in text selection seemed particularly significant. Jared commented, *"That was good. I like that 'cause I'm not a reader myself. I don't like reading, so being able to choose made it a little more enjoyable,"* and June explained, *"It was good to choose. We had to read* To Kill a Mockingbird. *It was boring, it just dragged on. It's dull, it didn't really have anything, no plot, nothing."*

As the group novel study progressed, students' interest levels remained high. They appeared more motivated to read their chosen novel than the class novel, and Meg was pleasantly surprised at the quality of the book talks the students gave in class. She commented that she hadn't believed they could be so insightful without much input from her as the teacher. The success of this small-group strategy seems to reinforce Patrick Dias's (1992a) notion that students can make their own meanings from texts when provided with an opportunity to engage with literature both independently and with their peers in class. Meg and I offered students some background information on the writers and on the setting of the novels, provided them with a strategy for addressing their particular topic of plot, theme, character, and writing style, and then left students alone to engage in individual reading and small-group discussions in class. Students who had completed their book early and had prepared their book talk ahead of others were offered another book by the same author or encouraged to self-select a book for class reading. After the book talks were completed, Meg encouraged students to consider how point of view in literary texts affects our reading of the text, and she focused students' attention on the different perspectives offered in the multicultural novels students had read.

In our personal interviews, students who chose to read *The Road to Memphis* noted the contrasting point of view with *To Kill a Mockingbird.* Jared explained,

> *I'm interested in black/white relations stories, It's kinda neat to know exactly what went on. In* The Road to Memphis *it was mainly the black side. It was how the blacks see it anyway.* To Kill a Mockingbird *was how the whites see the blacks... it was the same time zone. In* To Kill a Mockingbird *we just saw how they were treated, not how they feel or anything. With Cassie in the other book, she really told us what was going on.*

Farah commented,

> *The two books were pretty much on the same topic... they pretty much gave the same amount of respect to blacks in the books. Usually they are talking about a black person, but in* The Road to Memphis *they had a black person talking about what happened to their race, so I found that better and I liked it. Usually after I read a book like that it sticks in my mind and every time something happens, I recall it and I'll just flash back in my mind as I think, "Hey, I just read about that"... so it really does change me.*

Through reading contrasting texts with narrators from different racial and cultural backgrounds, and through classroom discussions on the importance of textual point of view, Farah and Jared are beginning to see the limitations of a text such as *To Kill a Mockingbird,* which, while appearing to promote an antiracist ideology, actually reinforces the position of power invested in white middle-class Western values. Reading the two contrasting novels helped these students to articulate and to challenge their own cultural values. As Gerald Graff (1992) points out, "Contrast is fundamental to understanding, for no subject, idea, or text is an island. In order to become intelligible 'in itself,' it needs to be seen in relation to other subjects, ideas, and texts" (108).

Other students, in their discussions with me about the novel they had selected to read, mentioned different literary texts their book brought to mind. Cathy told me:

> *I read* The Honorable Prison *and it reminded me of* The Endless Steppe *that I read last year. It's about a prison too, but set in Siberia....Also I thought about that story "The Non-revolutionaries" we read in class, it's also about people being prisoners in their homes, and they were taken over by Communist governments....There's lots of similarities really.*

And Brian said:

> *My novel was* Forbidden City. *That story we read before, set in Korea, they were fighting against their own people too, like Koreans against Koreans, and here it was Chinese against Chinese. This novel kept making me think of that story.*

Such comments reverberate with Bakhtin's (1984) notions of intertextuality, emphasizing the fluid interwoven boundaries between one's own words and the words of others. Students begin to see how texts are constructed like mosaics out of the texts of others, opening up potential for them to experience richness of language and the interconnections between literature and living.

Overall, Meg and I are pleased with the success of the small-group novel studies. Although students were only expected to read one of the four books offered to them, they had the opportunity to hear about the other three novels from students' book talks, and a number of students have since borrowed one of the other books from Meg to read in their own time.

Research Journal Entry: Tuesday, June 30

As the school year comes to a close, Meg and I have been able to reflect on our efforts to expand the literary canon in grade 10 classes and to address issues of representation in literary texts. Meg is encouraged by her students' responses to the new literature and determined to continue introducing postcolonial texts in subsequent classes. She acknowledges that not all the selected texts were good choices and will reconsider some of her selections in the future. She is uneasy about continuing with the film *Cry Freedom* because of its focus on the struggles of a white family and has decided not to use Gerry Weiner's speech on multiculturalism in future classes. Its didactic nature has tended to alienate students rather than helping them to look at their own involvement in issues of race and ethnicity. She will look more closely at translated texts to consider whether or not the translation interferes with the flow of the language. She is determined not to teach *To Kill a Mockingbird* again as a class study but will perhaps include it in students' choice of novels. Meg considers that of all the literature taught this year, Nadine Gordimer's story "Country Lovers" was the most successful in engaging students on a personal level and in helping them to begin to consider how issues of race, gender, class, ethnicity, and politics are inextricably intertwined. In the recent end-of-year exam in which students could choose to write on any text read this year, "Country Lovers" was the selection most commonly chosen by grade 10 students.

I believe that our efforts at canon expansion and our attempts to raise students' consciousness about all kinds of discrimination met with mixed success in the particular grade 10 class in which I was a participant observer. A number of these students willingly participated in this postcolonial pedagogy, coming to an increased understanding of the complexities of racism and intolerance, and beginning to acknowledge their own complicity in the structures of power. Others resisted becoming involved with the literature or with class discussions, revealing their discomfort with plurality and diversity. Many students come to class with their own ideologies firmly in place, and neither the power of literature nor the engagement of critical talk within the classroom will affect them. We have to make room within our classrooms for these responses, too. Jeff, for example, offered his own resistant reading of the texts in this class:

> What we're doing now is not of my highest interest, so I'm not sure there's too much I can contribute towards comments....Short stories, novels, and such things like that, I just don't have an interest in. Things such as poetry and philosophy are what I'm interested in...well, even then it depends on the subject of what I'm reading...all this racial discrimination stuff, it doesn't interest me. I mean, I have a concern towards it, but I don't need an English unit on it.

Such comments should not, I believe, discourage other teachers from attempting to move beyond the traditional Western texts they have traditionally offered students in their classes or to engage students in a new kind of critical pedagogy. They are simply a reminder that in a classroom setting, however successful a particular text or a particular strategy might appear to be with a majority of students, there will always be a minority who resist a teacher's attempt to introduce new ideas and to challenge students' existing ideological framework.

The visual images of this grade 10 English class engaged in reading and discussing postcolonial literature begin to fade as time goes by and both Meg and her students have moved on with their lives. Meg is now the English department head at the largest urban high school in the city, where students have a wide range of ethnocultural and linguistic backgrounds. Since our study ended, other teachers in Meg's former and current school and in other parts of her school district have expressed interest in the literature she taught during the time of my research, and have sought her advice on teaching strategies to use with the literature. Meg stresses the need to offer students choices of texts, to allow them opportunities to engage with literary texts both personally and communally in small group settings, and she cautions other teachers not to create a "new canon" of school texts that will simply replace the previous texts that were taught for so many years. She is aware that it is not enough for teachers simply to present students with different literature to read without making an effort to consider the importance of reading strategies that will interrogate the ideology of the texts.

Meg and I continue to search for postcolonial texts with possible appeal for adolescent readers, and she is continually updating her selections. The year after our study ended, her grade 10 students read the first chapter of Jamaica Kincaid's *Annie John,* and Meg read them excerpts from Maya Angelou's *I Know Why the Caged Bird Sings.* She has included more poetry from the Chinese-Canadian anthology *Many-Mouthed Birds,* is widening her novel selections to include works such as Sandra Cisneros's *The House on Mango Street,* and is looking for Native Canadian texts to include in her literary selections. Curriculum development such as this is never static but is an ongoing fluid process that acknowledges the diverse voices of students and the power of literature to engage hearts and minds.

Crossing Fictional Borderlands: *Obasan* and the Construction of Personal Identity

Spaces can be real or imagined. Spaces can tell stories and unfold histories. Spaces can be interrupted, appropriated, and transformed through artistic and literary practices.

bell hooks (1992, 153)

If we are interested in the ways in which history is lived, how it offers answers to the questions as to who we are and where we came from, if we want to know how we are produced as modern subjects, what narratives from the past enable us to construct identities, how historical memories and the shadows and ghosts of memories are internalised in our lives, then the "passions of identity politics" may drive us to ask new questions of old and new sources, fiction may give us necessary tools, the construction of new myths may be part of our work.

Catherine Hall (1996, 66)

In an attempt to move beyond a liberal notion of multiculturalism, which perceives cultural diversity as pre-given cultural contents and customs and invokes well-intentioned platitudes about prejudice and stereotype, I consider how any cultural system is constructed within a contradictory and ambivalent space that Homi Bhabha (1994) has identified as a "Third Space" (36). Here there is a continual historical and philosophical tension between political referents such as race, class, and gender and the discourses within which these categories are constructed.

In re-presenting my research study in Meg's grade 11 Advanced Placement (AP) class, I consider how the tensions of this "Third Space" enable students to interrogate the referents of race, class, and gender within the discourses of a particular literary text.

For many students in Canadian schools, painful tales of colonialism may seem mere myths from the past, and uncomfortable stories of discrimination toward immigrants and visible minorities may be dismissed as exaggerations or figments of oversensitive imaginations. Yet, for all students, remembrances of an imperial past may be vital if they are to help create a more compassionate future. "Memory," Catherine Hall (1996) notes, "is an active process which involves at one and the same time forgetting and remembering" (66). Such memories may often seem too painful to remember, but as Toni Morrison has shown in her novel *Beloved,* the past needs to be recovered through what she calls "rememory" if we are ever to come to terms with it and to embark on the construction of a more positive future.

Linked with notions of memory, of reconstructing the past, are questions of cultural identity. Catherine Hall posits that questions such as "Who are we?" "Where do we come from?" "Which 'we' are we talking about when we talk about 'we'?" have a particular salience in the contemporary classroom (66). Students today see themselves living in a shifting world with the break-up of old empires, the creation of new nations, and the movement of an unprecedented number of people across national and international boundaries.

Questions of roots and origins open up possibilities for teachers to explore with their students the complex and constructed nature of identity, to encourage students to see how knowledge is produced through language, and constantly being "re-written, re-cited and re-sited" (Chambers 1994a, 33). Identity in this view is not a static term, but a gendered, racialized, and historical construct that is constantly being formed and reformed in a cultural journey that is open and incomplete, with no fixed point of departure and no final destination. As we journey, we create our sense of self through a continual fabulation of the past and of the present, formulating what Chambers describes as "a particular story that makes sense" (26).

In Meg's grade 11 class, such questions of identities were explored through reading postcolonial literary texts that encouraged students to enter into dialogue with stories that intersected with their own. This cultural remapping opened up spaces for them to interrogate and to rethink the relationship between the powerful and the powerless and between themselves and others. These "pedagogical borderlands," Giroux (1992b) states, encourage a decentered perspective that allows students' own voices and experiences to intermingle with "particular histories that will not fit into the master narrative of a monolithic culture" (209).

Students in this class read a variety of postcolonial literature (see appendices), including short stories by V.S. Naipaul, Nadine Gordimer, and Abioseh Nicol, and poems by Michael Ondaatje and Atukwei Okai. It was Joy Kogawa's novel *Obasan,* however, that seemed to provide these students with the most powerful opportunity to engage in a critical reflection of their own identities. Students were asked to read *Obasan* during the summer, and then the novel was reread and discussed in class in conjunction with a number of Kogawa's poems dealing with the same historical period in her life.

In its exploration of a denied past, Kogawa's novel challenges its readers to come to terms with the blacked-out, repressed areas of national identity. Kogawa, born in Vancouver in 1935, describes herself as a *Nisei,* a second-generation Canadian. As a young child during World War II, she was evacuated with her family to Slocan, British Columbia, and later to Coaldale, Alberta. Her political activity within and for the Japanese-Canadian community permeates and informs her fiction and her poetry. She has become a voice for the Japanese-Canadian community, a role she has taken on with some ambivalence. For Kogawa, being a "hyphenated Canadian" has meant exclusion and loss. Through her writing, she seeks a new sense of reconciliation with her past:

> What is healing for a community is more than just a solution of a political kind. What heals is a process of empowerment; the process that heals is one where there is a striving for and an attainment of mutuality. (quoted in Hutcheon and Richmond 1990, 98)

In her novel *Obasan* (1983), Kogawa's childhood experiences are transformed and re-viewed through the eyes of the young child narrator, Naomi, seeking to rediscover the silenced stories of her family. These stories, replayed and reawakened in the memories of the old and in the letters of the dead, are, like the cultural stories of all human beings, fragmentary, complex, and contradictory:

> All our ordinary stories are changed in time, altered as much by the present as the present is shaped by the past. Potent and pervasive as a prairie dust storm, memories and dreams seep and mingle through cracks, settling on furniture and into upholstery. Our attics and living-rooms encroach on each other, deep into their invisible places. (25)

For Meg's high school students who read the novel, the stories in *Obasan* began to intermingle and weave through their own cultural histories and experiences. For some of these readers, the newly recognized narratives broke through barriers erected around familiar and safe fictions of the past, transforming and enriching them with new thoughts and experiences and opening up spaces for exploration. For others, who were perhaps less open to new ideas or more resistant to having their fictionalized worlds redefined, these new cultural stories were heard but not immediately recognized or acknowledged.

The complex individual experiences of each reader and text in the class were further complicated by the social context in which such textual encounters took place. As Britzman et al. (1993) remind us, "Classrooms are not hermetically sealed worlds." The larger school conditions "fashion the borders of interpretation and meaning" (190). They elaborate:

> [A]ddressing the controversies of our time means coincidentally a return to the contentions and deep investments of identity. "Selves" are neither made nor changed in isolation; the cost of identity entails reformulating the self with imperatives that, even while resisting the various forms of oppression, may still contradictorily veil and coincidentally assert how culture is lived as a relation of domination and subordination. The point is that sociality is governed by relations of power, and relations of power regulate the self. A central dilemma, then, of the slippery and shifting meanings of equity and difference concerns how individual and collective perspectives on these terms become implicated in larger discourses of social regulation. (190)

For many students in contemporary Canadian classrooms, the national fiction of Canada as a humane, nonracist, multicultural nation has permeated the construction of their own personal identities. Yet this fabulation is one not shared by all Canadians. For many Canadians of color, for example, living in Canada has meant living with racism and with experiences of exclusion.

Reading *Obasan* encouraged Bob, a white student with a German and Ukrainian heritage, to interrogate his previous vision of Canada as the home of equality and fairness. In a personal interview with me, following his reading of the novel, he explained:

> *Obasan triggers the same feelings and emotions of anger and sadness I felt when viewing the play* The Diary of Anne Frank. *However, it also induces an immense feeling of shock. We are not educated about this type of treatment which the Canadian country inflicted on our people. I call them "our" people, referring to the Japanese-Canadians, simply because they are in fact Canadians with a Japanese background, as I have Ukrainian and German backgrounds. After reading* Obasan *I am very perplexed about how a so-called "peace-keeping" country such as Canada could get away with such a thing. Was I one of many who was not aware of such horrific details, or do most know and not care? Stories such as this of any injustice handed down by my race, country, or ancestry make me ashamed. I should not feel this way....The author is trying to illustrate prejudice in a touching realistic situation by drawing the reader in to the actual life story of a victim. People as good as you or I are mis-*

*treated not because they do wrong things but because they simply look differ-
ent.*

Bob's reflections on his reading illuminate the contradictory and
fragile national and personal identities he has constructed from his previous history. Having apparently experienced no prejudicial treatment because of his own cultural heritage, he has created a fiction of "his
country" as a haven of tolerance and freedom. The voices of oppression
and marginality he recognized in his reading of *Obasan* forced him to
interrogate his previous assumptions. Bob's reading of this text and the
subsequent classroom discussions have opened up possibilities for a new
understanding of his own implications in the nation's history of forced
exclusions:

> *When I first began reading the book, I thought it was really hard to get through
> a lot of it. It seemed like there was a lot of information in it and stuff like that,
> that didn't really concern me much with the whole story, but when it came
> closer to the end, probably the last third of the book, everything came together
> and I was really impressed by how everything made sense....I felt even more
> strongly about the book after we had discussed it in class. I didn't know half of
> what they had in there about what happened in World War II with the Japanese
> and everything in Canada. I was really shocked to think that actually happened
> in Canada. I knew that some were relocated and stuff but I had no idea of all
> that poverty they were put into and all the hardships.*

Whereas Bob responded primarily to the descriptions of injustice in
the novel, other students in the same class engaged more with Kogawa's
evocative and poetic prose, which drew them into the experiences of her
fictional characters. Brenda, a white middle-class student with strong
Christian beliefs, was captivated by the metaphoric style of Kogawa's
writing.

> *I really loved* Obasan. *Some people find that books have to be really exciting
> for them, whereas the book that seems to have the least happening in it is the
> most exciting for me. I really enjoyed the style of writing itself; I don't think
> I've ever read a book so well written. I really liked the imagery and how Naomi
> said that her mother's leaving left a void in her life and that void solidified and
> became a wall of silence—you could see it all happening in your mind. I really
> enjoy books like that, that can keep me going up in my mind, rather than, you
> know, lots of action.*

Brenda explained that reading about Naomi's experiences of disempow-
erment in the novel and efforts to overcome the enforced silencing of her
family's history have led her to interrogate Christian values of compas-

sion and fairness that she had believed were shared by most Canadians. Brenda's reading raised important questions of power relations and authority in society and challenged her to explore the tension in knowledge created by a politics of remembrance:

> *Growing up, you slowly realize the world isn't perfect and that things do happen, but I think we can grow from this—like when you have people writing books and saying, "Hey, this really happened," it makes you try and sit back and think, "Well, what can we do to change this from happening in the future?"—and that's good; it's the way we learn and it helps a great deal.*

A number of students in this class had already been forced to recognize social conditions of inequality. Deanna, a quiet, thoughtful student with a mixed race heritage in the same grade 11 class, explained that she has personally encountered prejudice and racism within this inner-city school. Her reading of *Obasan* provided a wider context for her understanding of the uneven conditions of power and authority:

> *While reading Joy Kogawa's words, I felt anger, shock, pity, sadness, disgust, and admiration towards the situations and characters in the novel. I was both shocked and angry when I read how the Japanese-Canadians were forced off their own property, and their belongings as well as their livelihood given to the white race. I couldn't help but feel shame towards my country for claiming to be a multicultural democracy but underneath it was full of racial bigotry.... I think that everyone in the world would like to be strong and resilient like* Obasan, *but it is a very difficult task to accomplish especially when your own pain is crying out for attention.*

Deanna's reading of *Obasan* helped her to look more closely at the social and political production of equity and difference in Canada:

> *It made me think about Canada—they put the label that it's multicultural on it, to make it look all nice and friendly, but I think that everyone still considers it mostly British and French. Everyone in my generation thinks it's more multicultural than say the older generation. Like, we've got used to the fact that it's a country that's meant for different races. But the older generation didn't get that into their head. A lot of those people still think, "Oh, no! Canada is just British and French; that's what it is."*

For Deanna, reading *Obasan* opened up a world of new experiences and understandings that seemed to resonate with her own experiences of racism and simultaneously allowed her to gain insights into the problematic fictions she had constructed about national identity.

Other readers in this grade 11 class responded in different ways. A myth about classroom learning is that rationality leads to sensitivity and that learning is an orderly progression from ignorance to knowledge. This enlightenment view is subverted by the complex and contradictory realities of classroom life. As Meg found, teachers need to structure classroom discourse to make space for what Britzman (1991) terms "the unleashing of the unpopular" (60). For some students, reading postcolonial literature may have the effect of releasing their pain and anger as voices in the text connect with their own experiences. For Myka, a first-generation Canadian whose parents had moved to Canada from China, reading *Obasan* awakened painful family memories of war and destruction at the hands of Japanese soldiers. In his written response to Kogawa's book, he explained:

> *I felt infuriated reading this novel. The internment of the Japanese-Canadians is nothing compared to what they did in China. They killed 15 million people there. I would have been born in China instead of in Canada if they weren't there. I am not a racist, I just feel very bitter. That Aunt Emily in the novel really ticks me off. She shows Naomi all those documents about the "mistreatments." If she only knew about what her own race had done!*

In a subsequent interview with me, Myka expressed similar sentiments:

> *I feel sick over this incident with the Japanese Internment....It's nothing to what they were doing in Asia and to other island countries, and I'm sick that this is getting more attention than those earlier incidents....I won't talk about this in class though. It would be really hard to say what I felt, because other people might interpret my feelings as racist.*

Myka's responses, disturbing as they are in their manifestations of hate and bitterness, reveal the depth of feeling that postcolonial texts may evoke. Meg discovered that her attempts to initiate a postcolonial pedagogy raised issues not previously encountered in her more traditional literature classrooms. A pedagogy that hopes to transform reading strategies, that is structured to allow students to confront the ideologies of their own histories, needs to make room for such disturbing responses. As Stuart Hall (1991) suggests, when we teach about race, class, and gender, we create an atmosphere that allows people to say unpopular things:

> What I am talking about here are the problems of handling the racist timebomb and doing so adequately so that we connect with our students' experiences and can therefore be sure of defusing it. That experience has to surface in the class-

room even if it is pretty horrendous to hear; better to hear it than not because what you don't hear you can't engage with. (58–59)

Through whole-class and small-group discussions of *Obasan* and of Kogawa's poetry, and through personal writing opportunities, Meg continued to engage students in this grade 11 class in debates about issues of power and discrimination based on race, class, religion, and gender, about war and colonization and a need to confront such memories in order to ensure that they are not reinscribed in future histories. Myka said little in class, but he confronted me in the schoolyard two months after our initial talk to request another interview.

This time he explained:

> *Obasan got under my skin. I grew up with this hatred towards the Japanese, and I only wanted to hate them. You need an enemy sometimes to get through difficult times. After reading that novel and listening to what people had to say in class, I decided to read Kogawa's next novel* Itsuka. *It wasn't the same kind of fiction—it was a different book—more factual—so then I went to the library to get out other stuff to find out how true this was about the struggle the Japanese people had to get retribution. I feel a bit less bitter now. I realize it was the military, not the individual people who did those atrocities, but I do think it would be really worthwhile if the Chinese could get some retribution from the Japanese. I know that probably won't ever happen.*

Myka's reading of Kogawa's books opened up gaps in his previous constructions of knowledge, language, and identity that he brought with him into the classroom. What he inherited, as culture, as history, as language and tradition could not simply be erased from the story of his past. Rather, his sense of identity had been opened up for questioning by hearing other stories, other voices that placed him into an ambiguous space in which differences were permitted a hearing. Chambers (1994a) explains the potential of such encounters:

> If, as Benjamin, Wittgenstein and Heidegger insisted, we dwell in language, and its limits are the limits of our world, then to meet others within its fabric is to stretch it, double it, interrogate and remake it. It leads to a highly charged practice when we encounter diverse worlds, histories, cultures and experiences within an apparent communality. It is a meeting, a putting yourself on the line, that is invariably accompanied by uncertainty and fear. For it involves an encounter with a previous sense of self, of one's reason and certitude. (30)

For Myka, this entertaining of another sense of community appeared to weaken his ideas of the absolutism of his own cultural and national identity and encouraged him to move forward into a new zone that was open and full of gaps, irreducible to a single center or point of view.

The fragmentation of a homogenous and transcendental sense of our own identity and of the "other" shatters any reassuring fixed scheme of location and identity. Metaphors of migrancy and exile are replacing notions of a "metropolitan center" of the West, with the rest of world "out there." The figure of the traveler implies mobility and motion in both a metaphoric and a literal sense, a "willingness to go into different worlds, use different idioms, and understand a variety of disguises, masks and rhetorics" (Said 1991, 18). Abandoning fixed positions and ideologies of mastery "makes it possible to traverse different intellectual domains and explore a plurality of subject positions" (Behdad 1993, 43).

A postcolonial pedagogy that introduces students to new interrogatory reading strategies can enable individuals to break through the barriers enclosing the narrow confines of familiar territory within which they have created their own myths of national and personal identity. As students leave the confinement of their initial homes they become migrants, crossing borders of thought and experience with a new restless interrogation that can undo the terms of reference of their earlier existence. What makes this transformation possible is the shared medium of language.

Texts such as *Obasan* have the power to enable student readers to participate in conversations relating to conditions of knowledge, identity, and social relations. Classroom practice and discourse that are structured to make spaces for such engagements with texts, that address the ongoing, conflicting nature of social differences and attempt to deconstruct repressive ideologies of the past, have the potential to engage students in cultural re-mapping.

In this particular class, reading *Obasan* in the social context of the classroom allowed students such as Bob, Brenda, and Deanna to move toward new understandings of the fragility of identity as it travels through new landscapes intersected by a variety of languages and experiences. For some students who actively resist the voices in the text and refuse to engage in the ensuing classroom dialogue, discussions of race, class, and gender may have the effect of silencing their voices rather than encouraging them to be heard, and there may not appear to be any new understandings. However, as my story of Myka suggests, creating new spaces for students to recognize the multilayered and contradictory ideologies that construct their own identities and to question differences within and between various groups may have surprising results.

Localities of the Everyday:
Pedagogical Perspectives

Beyond the edges of the map we enter the localities of the vibrant everyday world and the disturbance of complexity.

Iain Chambers (1994a, 92–93)

While the wholesale re-envisioning of society remains incomplete, few of us have any trouble envisioning the work that awaits us as scholars and educators. The picture is daunting and exciting. It is not necessary to dream to encounter scholars and teachers excited by new possibilities for understanding, driven by curiosity, eager to read the lost texts and the new ones, eager to branch out of their specializations and to devise forms of collaborative work that are accountable to heterogeneity and multiplicity.

Mary Louise Pratt (1996, 19)

For many well-intentioned English teachers who applaud the idea of a postcolonial literary education for their students, the day-to-day constraints of teaching soon dampen their enthusiasm. As Susan, a young English teacher in a multiethnic American school, quickly discovered, the trivia of teaching can easily overwhelm good intentions: "I began teaching. The meaning of multicultural education soon was washed over by the daily concerns of learning names, assigning reading, checking homework, and keeping things semi-orderly" (Mizell et al. 1993, 30).

Arthur Applebee (1993), in his studies of literature teaching in American junior and senior high schools, found that teachers were confused about how to go about reinventing their curriculum. He explains:

What is lacking is a well-articulated overall theory of the teaching and learning of literature, one that will give a degree of order and coherence to the daily decisions that teachers make about what and how to teach. Such a theory is needed to place the various critical traditions into perspective, highlighting the ways in which they can usefully complement one another in the classroom, as well as the ways in which they are contradictory. (202)

Teachers, he writes, want answers to such basic questions as "What text should we choose?" "How should we decide what questions to ask about a literary work?" and "How should a student's response be followed up?" and they want their questions revisited within a more comprehensive theoretical framework (202).

Bruce Goebel and James Hall (1995) make a similar argument about the need for teachers to understand pedagogical approaches that will help them to initiate curricular changes:

> [T]heorists of culture and democracy have succeeded in identifying and articulating much of the problematics regarding race, gender and social class, but they have failed to create a corresponding pedagogical technology—largely because they have failed to account for the social dynamics of real classrooms. Recent pedagogical specialists, from writing process advocates to reader-response theorists, have concretely outlined practical classroom methods but have failed to adequately connect them to contemporary debates regarding the relationship among a literary education, cultural diversity and democracy. (xiv)

What is needed perhaps, in order to understand the complex interactions among students, teachers, texts, and theories are studies and writing that acknowledge the links between theory, interpretation, and the art of teaching and also accept that classrooms are messy places, lacking the utopian tidiness that characterizes much writing about teaching.

In reflecting on our collaborative research study, Meg and I attempted to come to terms with some of this messiness of teaching, accepting that when we initiate a pedagogy that seeks to legitimize multiple traditions of knowledge and to affirm the voices of the marginalized, that challenges outdated notions of curriculum practice with respect to race, class, culture, and gender, there will be countless new challenges for both teachers and students to face. In addition, the demands of a skills-based curriculum are very much in evidence in schools, with administrators and parents wanting teachers to be accountable for their students' academic achievements. For many English teachers, meeting all of these demands may seem daunting at best and often overwhelming.

When I interviewed Meg, in the summer following the completion of our research study, about her efforts to introduce new literature into her classes and to initiate a postcolonial pedagogy, she was very positive about the work:

It was a really good experience. It rejuvenated me. The idea of trying new things was wonderful. I'm very keen to get back into it again. Last year I was just feeling my way all the time thinking, "Is this going to work?" This year I have much more confidence going in with it. I will be able to spend more time looking at the literature and how to teach it and I think it will be fine.

When I asked Meg if she thought her students had benefited from reading the postcolonial literature, she explained that their reactions were generally positive, that they were pleased to see the literature, and interested in literature by people around the world.

I discussed with Meg comments that her students had made in our interviews. Some students in grade 11 told me they were shocked to find that they were implicated in some kind of social arrangement that was racist or classist and that they hadn't realized that Canadian society itself was a participant in this. Meg felt that it was time for students to understand their own histories:

I think that's important for them to know—that yes, we have been participants in this ugliness. I think that's what they saw. It's one of our twentieth-century shames. I think we all need to know that. Not that we want them just to feel anger and despair at what's happened either but we need to get involved, not just read the Hollywood version of stories and believe those.

When I asked Meg if she had noticed any differences between the responses of her white students and her minority students to the new literary texts, she responded:

I think the immigrant or international students engaged much more with the literature. They gained more comfort from it perhaps than my Caucasian students did. Although that's certainly not true with everyone. I think at the grade 12 level there was a more even response to it than at the grade 10 and 11, and maybe that's just maturity, but I think that the immigrant students engaged more quickly with the literature, they appreciated it more, were happy to see it, and with the numbers of immigrant and minority students we have, who've been shuffled aside so long, it's time they were given some consideration.

I was interested in knowing whether Meg would teach the same literature if she were teaching at a different school with predominantly white students, accepting the fact that some of them might be resistant to reading postcolonial texts. Meg was quite emphatic in her response:

I would, even if there were some discomfort with it, I don't think that's a bad thing either. Some of our students said they felt shame and embarrassment at some of the situations, and that they had been part of this. I think that's good to feel that discomfort, that they can really see how they can make a difference. I think they need to know the world is much bigger than Alberta, and the world is much bigger than Canada or America, and that good literature comes from other places. I think that's really important. I know some students didn't like the literature being called "antiracist." I think next year, I won't label it "anti-racist" literature. I'll just call it international literature. Or maybe I won't label it at all. We love our labels and maybe that was a problem for some students.

When I asked Meg if she could identify some of the hurdles and problems she had encountered during the year in trying to expand the literary canon, she responded:

I think the hardest part of it was that I wasn't well enough planned. I found that I was doing a lot of things the night before, and I hadn't thought it through enough. There's no way round that when you're doing something new. It was a really good experience, but it was also a tense experience, thinking, "Have I got enough done?" "Is this right?" Now that I've got some good reactions to this, it will be an easier year from that point of view and perhaps a better year. That was probably the most difficult. I could have used more time.

She also explained that not everything she had attempted had been successful:

I think I tried to teach too many short stories, too much literature. I think what I needed to do was give the kids more time to think about it. When I look at the number of stories that we've gone through and the amount of literature we've actually been studying, I see questions and concerns that still need to be addressed. With different classes it's different. I found with my grade 11 Advanced Placement class, I could take a lot longer to look at a story than I could with my 10s because of their interest level. I think I wasn't aware of how weak some of my 10s were to start with. I need to take that into account too when I decide on the amount I can ask them to do and the amount I ask them to read. I'll definitely use the novels again. I think that was a success story for sure. Offering choice was a winner—that came through time and time again. I didn't do as well with the poetry selections. I need to look for more poetry for next year.

Meg also expressed a concern about the quality of the translations of some of the selected literature:

I do think the quality of the literature is very important. I'm thinking back to the Chinese story "Love Must Not Be Forgotten" that was so difficult to read aloud. It didn't work as well because it didn't read as well. Not one student chose to write on that text in the exam. I wouldn't teach that this year, although I enjoyed the story. It didn't seem as appropriate for the grade 10s and I do think it was a poor translation.

I was curious about Meg's reaction to other teachers asking for copies of the new literature and for her teaching notes. She explained that she was happy to share any of the texts but she had reservations about other teachers simply trying to duplicate her teaching without any personal commitment or theoretical framework for teaching the literature:

> Now that I've got some of the work done, I can hand it on to them and it would then be a lot easier for them and, in fact, that's what has been happening this year already. But I do think it's important to do the selecting yourself too, because that's part of the process of learning what's happening with the literature, and what's happening with your kids when you teach it. I have some hesitation in just handing it over because I don't know if there's ownership on the teacher's part. On the other hand, I'd like to have the literature taught. I know that there are people who just take it wholesale—take it down and photocopy it, but they would do that with anything. The situation is more complicated, however, than just teaching the literature. I'll have to think more about this.

In our subsequent conversation we discussed the difficulties many teachers have in moving away from considering themselves as the "expert reader" in the classroom. Meg agreed that it would be more difficult for such teachers to introduce postcolonial literature to their students. Meg's own teaching philosophy enabled her to create a dialogic classroom in which she and her students formed a community of readers and learners:

> I guess I don't think I'm the expert reader. If I thought I were an expert I wouldn't value my students as much or respect how they're coming to the literature. Some of them see so much more than I do and I'm happy to acknowledge that—that's what makes it really interesting for me. It can be more of a dialogue then rather than a teaching of the literature and I would far rather have a dialogue with my students about the literature than think I can hold the answers. That's just something that doesn't interest me. I certainly know I'm the more experienced reader, and it would not be truthful if I said anything different, but I don't see myself as the expert and my students don't either. At times I know it's frustrating on their part, when they ask a question and I say, "I don't understand this," or, "I don't know this; let's look at this again." They look at me askance, but I don't think that lasts for long either. I think the more secure they feel in their own interpretation, the better readers they will become. If they're just going to sit back and wait till someone tells them what the literature is about they're not going to engage. That doesn't interest me.

In our discussion on reading strategies, Meg emphasized the importance of allowing students to read and to discuss the literature in small groups with their peers. I explained that in my interviews with students, it was predominantly minority students who commented on the value of small-group discussions, but Meg felt that they were valuable for all students:

> Yes, it's important but not just for my international students either. I think Caucasian students as well. In fact it's only been my Caucasian students who've ever refused to do presentations or speak out in class, and I think that's really interesting. I know the international students are really appreciative of small groups and hate to speak out publicly, but I think it's important for all students to have that small-group interaction right from the beginning through to the end.

She stressed that groups need to be well-designed so that everyone has the opportunity to participate:

> Sometimes the Caucasian students need to be separate from the international students, just because the international students will speak more freely, particularly if they're all Chinese in one group for example. But I think it's important to spread them around too, so that they can share their feeling one-on-one or one-on-three or whatever, so we need to design our groups with that in mind.

In Applebee's (1993) studies of the literature taught in American schools, teachers expressed concerns about community approval of their selected literature. I was interested to know whether Meg had received any feedback from parents or from other members of the community about the international texts she had been teaching. She explained:

> I didn't feel pressure, but I certainly had interest. Parents who came to the parent-teacher interviews in November talked about some of the literature and I was really pleased to see that. They mentioned some of the short stories, particularly in grade 10. The Japanese story "Swaddling Clothes" was one of the texts parents had read and were really interested in talking about. So, if anything, there was interest and support. Some parents said it was really good to see that their children didn't have to read the same stories they had had to read in school.

Meg explained that what had made the changes feasible for her was the support she had received from her department head and the assistance that I had been able to offer in text selection and during the teaching of the literature.

> I couldn't have done it unless you had been doing all that work every day. First of all I wouldn't have known where to go for the literature and I wouldn't have had the resources you found for me. For example, the anthology *Multicultural Perspectives* was such a wonderful find.

Bearing in mind that not all teachers would be able to develop a similar collaborative relationship with a researcher, I asked Meg what kinds of support systems might enable other teachers to embark on making canonical changes in their literature teaching and to initiate a form of postcolonial pedagogy. Meg explained that she felt it was necessary for teachers to be enthusiastic about making changes in their literary selections and to see a need to move beyond traditional forms of teaching strategies that supported reading Western canonical texts to the exclusion of non-Western and minority literature. In addition, she pointed to the need for university courses and teacher education courses to support changes and for additional teaching resources:

> When I think back to when I first taught English, I remember that Canadian literature wasn't taught very much either until there were university courses for support and there were anthologies with Canadian literature in them and with some background support for teaching it. I think of the anthologies we still use at the grade 12 level, like *Story and Structure.* There's nothing in there for teaching international literature. Until we have different anthologies, it will be too difficult, there's no question.

Reflecting on Dasenbrock's (1992) theory that teachers can approach unfamiliar postcolonial texts as "a scene of learning" without any background material or knowledge, I was interested in Meg's perceptions about this issue. Although she considered that much of the literature seemed to stand alone quite well, Meg conceded that she felt more comfortable introducing a text to students when she had some contextual information about the writer or about the setting:

> As teachers, we don't even know about these authors. We just don't. I would not have known about them at all if you hadn't been there giving them to me, saying "Try this." "This might work." I like to have the background knowledge for myself. Not that I feel I always have to give it to my students but I do like to have it. I think it has to come. When I see a newer literary anthology such as *Literary Experiences,* it's certainly predominantly North American and British, but it has some international selections and I think that's a starting point for new anthologies. I think publishers are aware that teachers need more variety—it's starting to happen. But certainly more needs to be done.

Meg admitted that with current cutbacks in school resource budgets, it might be difficult for teachers to gain access to new materials. She was optimistic, however, that as more teachers returned to university and discovered international literature for themselves and encountered new reading and teaching strategies that acknowledged the diversity of students in classrooms, the situation in schools might begin to change.

Today, a number of years after the study, Meg remains enthusiastic about the work of canon expansion in her school, and is constantly seeking new literature and new ways of acknowledging the cultural diversity of her students. As Meg's interest and involvement in a postcolonial pedagogy have deepened, she has gained an increased awareness of the complexities of curriculum reform and the need to look beyond text selection to the more intricate issues implicit in creating spaces for the multiplicity of voices waiting to be heard in our classrooms.

In our most recent discussion, Meg echoed the words she spoke in our previous interview: "The situation is more complicated than just teaching the texts." Although increasingly convinced of the value of introducing international literature to her students, she expressed her concerns about the impact, if any, that reading postcolonial literature has on students' view of the world and on how they live in the world. This is a crucial question with particular relevance for this kind of research. In our discussion, Meg wondered whether increasing incidents of racially motivated violence in her school could be addressed in any positive way by introducing students to postcolonial literature and challenging them to interrogate the discourses of race, class, and gender that inform the texts and curriculum practice. These are vital questions for the future. Does literature taught in school have any transformative power in the world outside the text? Can a postcolonial pedagogy effect changes in a student's consciousness or merely raise students' awareness of the inequalities of power structures in the world?

Maxine Greene (1995) suggests that if we are appreciative of storytelling as a mode of knowing and of the connection between narrative and the ambivalent shaping of identity, then we should believe that literary engagement can help us to make connections with our own lives and experiences:

> [T]his awareness of the significance of story, and of understanding rather than mere conceptualization, seems to have led a number of educators and others to inquiries in which the perspectives of the human sciences are deepened and expanded by imaginative literature. I have recalled, for example, how we may read about the history, demographics, and economics of slavery in this country, but we may also read Toni Morrison's *Beloved,* and in the course of achieving it as meaningful, find ourselves possessing a new perspective of slavery, perhaps also a stunned outrage, perhaps also more about our own lives and experiences of loss even as we perceive more about the world of slavery once we are enabled to look at it through our own lived situations. (186–87)

As Greene (1995) acknowledges, there is still a place for historical description of past events, but engagement with literature enables readers to tap into new circuits of reader consciousness and to make connections with our own lives and times:

> We begin moving beyond immediacies and general categories, as reflective practitioners are bound to do when they try to make sense. We see; we hear; we make connections. We participate in some dimensions that we could not know if our imagination were not aroused....Having accepted "unreality," we can turn them back to the variegated social realities we share and, perhaps, find them enhanced, expanded, corrigible. (186–87)

Will any of Meg's students experience a "stunned outrage" about racist behavior after imaginatively sharing the experiences of Cassie and her brothers in *The Road to Memphis,* or of Lena in Nadine Gordimer's "Happy Event"? Will this changed consciousness enable them to find their social reality "enhanced, expanded, corrigible"? These are among the many unanswered questions of my study.

Revisioning the Journey
of Postcolonial Pedagogy

Travel, in both its metaphorical and physical reaches, can no longer be considered as something that confirms the premises of our initial departure, and thus concludes in a confirmation, a domestication of the difference and the detour, a homecoming. It is caught up in a wider itinerary which poses the perspective of an interminable movement, and with it questions connected to a lack of being placed, to the proposal of perpetual displacement.

Iain Chambers (1994b, 246)

Art is a way into other realities, other personalities. When I let myself be affected by a book, I let into myself new customs and new desires. The book does not reproduce me, it re-defines me, pushes at my boundaries, shatters the palings that guard my heart. Strong texts work along the borders of our minds and alter what already exists.

Jeanette Winterson (1996, 26)

A journey may be considered as a metaphor for narrative, as a process of development, growth, and change and a physical movement that usually involves a leaving and a return. The quest motif in many traditional Western narratives sees travelers leaving home on a journey of self-discovery, encountering obstacles along the way, learning from their experiences, and returning home having gained wisdom and maturity. In a postcolonial, poststructuralist narrative, travel is less linear, more fragmented. As Chambers (1994b) suggests, "the journey outwards towards other worlds today reveals an uncertain journey inwards: an expedition that exposes tears in the maps and a stammer in the languages we in the West have been accustomed to employ" (245). Like the narrative of this book, a postmodern journey is winding and heterogeneous with hybrid elements interrupting the passage. Travelers' hopes of eventual arrival and homecoming are disrupted and subject to perpetual displacement. Utopian dreams of the pleasures of travel are replaced by the ambiguities of exile, of migrancy, and of diasporic identities. Chambers (1994b) explains:

> To think, to write, to be, is no longer for some of us simply to follow on the tracks of those who initially expanded and explained our world as they established the frontiers of Europe, of Empire, and of manhood, where the knots of gendered, sexual and ethnic identity were sometimes loosened, but more usually tightened. Nor is it surely to echo the mimicries of ethnic absolutisms secured in the rigid nexus of tradition and community, whether in nominating our own or others' identities. It is rather to abandon such places, such centres for the migrant's tale, the nomad's story. It is to abandon the fixed geometry of sites and roots for the unstable calculations of transit. (246)

Travelers on this postmodern journey depart with their own baggage in hand, with differing senses of place, of language, of culture and history. As they travel they begin to understand that culture, rather than being a "stronghold of separate traditions, autonomous histories, self-contained cultures and fixed identities," is fluid and flexible, capable of transformation and translation (Chambers 1994b, 247). As travelers engage in dialogue with other voices, both textual and personal, they begin to acknowledge the transforming potential of hybridity, recognizing the place of others in the world and reconsidering the existing languages of culture, identity, and power that have served as divisions in the world. Such a decentering of knowledge, language, and identity reinforces Salman Rushdie's claim that "we are increasingly becoming a world of migrants, made up of bits and fragments from here, there. We are here. And we have never left anywhere we have been" (in Burton 1992, 122).

Like many others in Canada, I am a Canadian citizen who has lived in different countries before settling here. I have spoken different languages and different dialects of English, been part of different cultures and traditions. All my experiences have contributed to my sense of being and becoming. I have been fortunate in that, since coming to Canada, I have always been accepted as a Canadian, have experienced no sense of rejection because of my background. Others, predominantly visible minorities in Canada, have been less fortunate. Jan Wong, the Canadian journalist and author, has written about her experiences of returning to Canada from a reporting assignment and finding herself detained for hours in immigration at Toronto's Pearson Airport. No one would admit why she had been selected for interrogation, nor could anyone find any problems with her Canadian passport. Wong comments:

> We are a nation of immigrants, but not all our ancestors had white skin. My family has been here for 111 years. Family lore has it that my maternal grand-

father, who helped to build the railway that linked our country together, was the 10th Chinese to become a Canadian citizen back around 1898. How long does it take to become a full-blooded Canadian? Two hundred years? Three hundred years? (Wong 1996, D1)

Wong's experiences highlight the importance of moving away from ideas of the universality and fixity of meanings toward an acceptance of the values of migrancy and heterogeneous identities, and an openness to different ways of being and knowing. My research study has explored ways to promote such openness through a postcolonial pedagogy that attempts simultaneously to offer students opportunities to engage with postcolonial texts that may resonate with their own cross-cultural backgrounds and experiences, and to create possibilities for interrogating and deconstructing representations of self, place, and others in literary texts.

I set out on this research journey with three primary questions in mind: to consider both the positive and negative values for students from diverse cultural backgrounds of reading postcolonial texts in school, to look at the potential of a postcolonial pedagogy for deconstructing misrepresentations of the "other" in both canonized and newer international literature, and to gain insights into the challenges and difficulties faced by a high school teacher attempting to initiate such a pedagogy in a multiethnic high school. Other questions emerged throughout the journey as I considered issues of text selection (Smagorinsky 1995, Greenlaw 1994), pondered dilemmas arising from efforts to translate theory into practice in the classroom (Wolff 1996, Naidoo 1992, Spears-Bunton 1990), and debated questions of textuality, representation, translation, and border crossing arising from my own research. As I attempt to grapple with all these issues, I acknowledge immediately that my study is able at best to offer only partial insight into a number of these questions, and in some cases simply raises further questions for future studies.

In my collaborative study with Meg, we discovered that students from minority backgrounds gain particular benefits from reading postcolonial literature in school. The responses of these students in all three grades of Meg's school to reading postcolonial texts that affirmed their voices in the classroom were overwhelmingly positive. Such texts did not need to be set in the particular cultural milieu of individual students in order to resonate with their own histories, traditions, and experiences. Nina, a Native Canadian student in Meg's grade 12 class, spoke eloquently of the power of Nadine Gordimer's South African story "Happy Event" to bring to the forefront issues of racism that she had encountered in her daily life. She commented too that the islanders' fear of difference in the García Márquez story "A Very Old Man with Enormous Wings," which led them to treat the old man so badly, reminded her of Canadians' lack of understanding of Native peoples and traditions. She believed that students should be reading these kinds of literary texts that "have something to do with us."

Karen, an immigrant from Vietnam, considered that the young girl in Amy Tan's story "Two Kinds" shared many of her own cultural confusions and she felt that stories about clashes between cultures were particularly meaningful for her because of her own cross-cultural situation. She saw too that the gender issues foregrounded in Ferré's story "The Youngest Doll" were relevant to her own experiences and background. Kwan, another Vietnamese immigrant, loved Amy Tan's essay "Mother Tongue" because it commented on the kinds of language difficulties and expectations that she has had to face at home and at school. Kien, who was also born in Vietnam, explained that the cross-cultural problems experienced by the girl and her mother in "Two Kinds" resonated with the different expectations he and his parents have for his future.

Students in the grade 11 class in our study also commented on the positive values of reading postcolonial literature in class. Deanna, who described herself as having a "mixed-race heritage," explained that reading Kogawa's novel *Obasan* made her want to be strong and resilient against racial bigotry but that she found such a response difficult because of her "own pain." She felt that reading Kogawa's novel and poetry had offered her new insights into her own experiences. Myka, the Chinese-Canadian student whose initial responses to *Obasan* were resentment and anger at the novel's focus on discrimination against Japanese-Canadians, found that reading Kogawa's poetry in school and her novel *Itsuka* at home enabled him to gain a more balanced perspective on the destructive forces of prejudice and racism.

Meg had already witnessed the discomfort of her students from Asian backgrounds at having their cultural experiences made the focus of class discussion and she was subsequently wary of teaching literature that might expose aspects of her students' culture they preferred to keep hidden. In our collaborative study, we were careful to select texts from a variety of countries and cultures, seeking to stress the heterogeneous and cross-cultural aspects of the literature. Students seemed much more at ease in these classes and more open to debating issues of culture, race, and gender that emerged in particular texts. The grade 12 students with Asian backgrounds were particularly vocal in discussions on the mother-daughter relationship in Amy Tan's "Two Kinds." Many of these students decided to read *The Joy Luck Club,* from which the story is excerpted, as well as *The Kitchen God's Wife.* In my interviews with several grade 12 students from Chinese backgrounds, they overwhelmingly supported the inclusion of texts such as "Two Kinds" in the syllabus and a number spoke of the value of reading literature "about people like me." In the year following our study, Meg included a novel study of *The Joy Luck Club* in her curriculum and offered students opportunities to critique the film of the book.

This research suggests that there are advantages for students from minority backgrounds in reading postcolonial texts with an evocative appeal to aspects of their own histories and experiences. Yet the study also points to the dangers of stereotyping minority students from particular cultural backgrounds by expecting them to speak as "representatives" of their culture. It became clear in Meg's classrooms that while some students from minority backgrounds seemed willing to engage in whole-class discussions about their experiences, others preferred to talk only in small groups with their peers and to make their own decisions about how much to expose their personal backgrounds. Yet others preferred to comment on their cultural experiences in personal writing assignments. Meg's teaching strategies allowed students the freedom to make such choices.

This study also affirms the potential value of reading postcolonial literature for students from mainstream backgrounds. Aronowitz and Giroux (1991) claim that postcolonial texts "provide another language and voice by which other students can understand how differences are constructed, for better or worse, within the dominant curriculum" (101) and that these texts "offer all students forms of counter-memory that make visible what is often unrepresentable in many English classrooms" (102). Tymoczko (2000) believes that "postcolonial texts are communicative agents with powerful resonances, having the capacity to mediate between languages and cultures in radical and empowering ways" (148). These critics point to the need for all students to cross borders that are constructed within discourses of race, gender, class, and nation. Both Meg and I entered the research with the intention of raising students' awareness of the overlapping terrains of knowledge and power, and we attempted to provide a context for students to cross such borders.

Students in grade 12 in our study were encouraged to consider how essentialist notions of racial identities, of class, gender, religion, and culture can lead to incidents of prejudice, racism, and misunderstandings in their readings of Gordimer's "Happy Event," García Márquez's "A Very Old Man with Enormous Wings" and Ferré's "The Youngest Doll." Our subsequent efforts to engage students in a critical dialogue with one another about these issues in the texts provided a context for these border crossings. Similarly, grade 11 students who were reading Kogawa's novel and poems engaged in critical assessments of their country's collaboration in a political regime that, only a generation ago, forcibly removed a segment of Canada's population from their homes and interned them because of their ethnic affiliations. For many of these students, such knowledge awakened them to an understanding that even in a supposedly humane country such as Canada, there is potential for stereotyping people because of their race, gender, or ethnicity. Similar themes emerged in students' reading of V.S. Naipaul's short story "B. Wordsworth" (about a black Caribbean poet), Abioseh Nicol's "The Judge's Son" (a story of destructive pride set in Sierra Leone), and Nadine Gordimer's "Another Part of the Sky" (a complex South African story of a reform-school headmaster's misguided priorities).

In grade 10, the selected postcolonial short stories and poetry offered students opportunities to recognize and analyze how racism, prejudice, and fear of difference can shut out understanding and create divisions between people. It was clear from the study that some texts have more potential than others to engage students on an emotional and personal level. Whereas students spoke in an indirect way of their interest in issues of racism through reading Gerry Weiner's speech "Youth Our Best Hope to End Racial Discrimination" and viewing the film *Cry Freedom,* they engaged in a more direct and personal way with the experiences of Thebedi and Paulus in Nadine Gordimer's story "Country Lovers." Through discussing and writing about this story, many students began to consider the socially constructed nature of the categories "black" and "white" within an institutionalized discourse of racism.

In their small-group novel studies, grade 10 students also began to interrogate point of view in texts and to see the limitations of viewing the world through one particular lens. Students noticed how Scout's white middle-class viewpoint in Lee's novel *To Kill a Mockingbird* limits readers' perspectives on black culture and experiences. Although portrayed with compassion in the novel, African-American experiences are nevertheless designated as ineffectual and inferior compared with those of whites. Students were able both to engage on a personal level with literature and to see narratives as "highly organized, structured discourses that may deliberately advocate particular social practices or implicitly encode such practices" (Johnston 1996, 108). Such recognitions may be the first step in helping readers to deconstruct representations of race, gender, class, and culture in literary texts.

Many of Meg's students were willing participants in such analysis and deconstruction. Marlene, for example, reading *To Kill a Mocking-*

bird, questioned Scout's comments that in Calpurnia's church there was "a clean Negro smell" (117), asking why Scout would think that black people had a different smell. "Wasn't that a racist remark?" queried Marlene. Another student, Jared, commented that in *To Kill a Mockingbird* "it was how the whites see the blacks...we just saw how they were treated, not how they feel or anything," and Farah noted that in Lee's novel, as in most books she had read, "they are talking about a black person."

Other grade 10 students, however, although they spoke of the value of choice offered them in selecting a novel to read, had little to say about their selected book and even less about the short stories they had read. These students were either unwilling or unable to articulate, either in personal interviews or in their writing, how the texts had connected with their own lives or whether reading the literature had helped them to recognize reductionist stereotypes in other texts they had read. With the invisibleness of the reading process we can never know for sure how these students responded to the literature. Students such as Jeff who commented that "all this racial discrimination stuff" was of no interest to him, and Colin who fell asleep in class probably gained little from reading the literature or from our efforts to create a context for them to connect the literature with their own lives and views of the world.

From a teaching perspective, re-mapping literary worlds in the classroom and initiating a postcolonial pedagogy can be challenging. Canadian teachers, although constrained by provincial mandates to teach certain genres of literature, have traditionally had more freedom to introduce students to a wide range of literature than I did in South Africa in the 1970s. Yet, as evidenced by Applebee's (1989, 1990) studies of teachers in the United States, and Cameron's (1989) and Altmann, Johnston, and Mackey's (1998) studies of teachers in Western Canada, North American teachers are reluctant to move beyond teaching the familiar texts they themselves read in school and university. Even with reassurances that the inclusion of literature by minority writers in the curriculum offers potential to address the interests of all their students, many teachers will find it difficult to make changes without institutional support. When available resources are inadequate, selecting unfamiliar postcolonial texts accessible to a range of high school readers requires hours of preliminary reading. Researching background material on authors and on the literature adds to the workload. Although I assisted Meg with the selection of texts and with the development of curricular materials, the day-to-day preparation and lesson planning were Meg's responsibility. She was fortunate in having the support of her department head, who had already taught a number of international texts in his own classes and was agreeable to including the purchase of new anthologies in the school budget. In addition, Meg's principal and the school librarians encouraged her endeavors to expand her literary selections, and she was able to use the library budget for the purchase of new novels for the grade 10 small-group novel study.

Despite having the support of her colleagues and a researcher, Meg received little practical assistance in her actual teaching. She found that lack of time was a primary concern, as she worked every evening to plan her teaching for the following day and often rushed in to school early in the morning to photocopy material for students. I was not able to be in class every day because of commitments at university, so although I assisted in material preparation, I did little of the actual work involved in teaching the new literature at three different grade levels. Because Meg is an experienced teacher with a large repertoire of teaching strategies and has a passion for new ideas and new literature, she was able to make the transition to teaching unfamiliar texts in her classes. Occasionally, however, the stress of attempting so many new things in a particular time frame was apparent. One day I came late to Meg's grade 10 class to find her students engrossed in discussing Jim Wong-Chu's poem "Equal Opportunity" and considering why the poet had chosen to conclude his poem in such an enigmatic way. When students settled down to a writing assignment, I quietly asked Meg why she had given students only half the poem to read. We discovered to our great amusement that she had mislaid the second page of the photocopy that I had given her and had assumed the poem was complete in its one-page version. Rather than allowing students to remain oblivious of her error, she explained to them what had happened and the class proceeded to discuss the poem in its "new" format.

Meg's response to this incident is indicative of her honesty and willingness to show her students that she is not infallible. In many other ways, she displayed her interest in being a co-learner with her students in the reading of postcolonial literature. Rather than perceiving herself as an authorized reader whose authority directs and subverts student inquiry, Meg is willing "to shed the mantle of the expert, the role of final mediator between the reader and the text" (Dias 1992a, 159) and to allow students to come to their own understandings of a text. She encourages students to discuss literature in small-group formats and to accept responsibility for the meanings they make from literature. When she offered students contextual information on a particular text, for example in her teaching of "The Non-revolutionaries," she sought ways to engage students in the discussion by relating to their personal spheres of knowledge through her discussion of the television series *M*A*S*H*. Students were then encouraged to bring their own experiences and background knowledge to the discussion. Rather than simply adding historical facts to the text, Meg promoted an intertextual engagement. Her approach to teaching creates a classroom compatible with Bakhtin's (1981) notion of a "dialogic environment" where there is room for a "living mix of varied and opposing voices" (xxviii).

Meg's students from minority backgrounds particularly valued the opportunity to discuss their responses to literature in small groups; many of them explained in personal interviews that they found it difficult and intimidating to speak in a whole-class setting. A number of Meg's students from mainstream backgrounds also commented on the value of discussing literature with a small number of their peers. Diana in grade 10 explains what she considers to be the value of small-group discussions:

> If you're in a small group you can exchange ideas, and if you don't understand something, maybe one of your partners can give you the concept of the thing. It's good because you get to learn more and that. You know, you work together, you're more comfortable working together and instead of going up and asking the teacher, you can talk to your friends.

Meg acknowledges that for some of her students her approach to teaching literature may be frustrating, as they expect her to have ready-made answers for all their questions on a particular text, to be what Dasenbrock (1992) describes as the "already informed interpreter" of the literature read in school (36). In one grade 12 class, for example, where students were studying Ferré's complex story "The Youngest Doll," a student approached Meg after class to express his concern that she had chosen to teach a story which she "didn't really understand properly" herself. Meg concedes that for teachers with more prescriptive teaching styles, implementing changes to the canon may be far more demanding than it was for her.

For many teachers, already burdened with larger class sizes, less marking time, increasing pressures for accountability, and additional standardized testing, the extra demands of implementing curriculum changes may seem daunting. Such changes may be feasible only over a period of time with the development of new teaching resources, changes in teacher education programs that encourage students and teachers to take courses on international literature and postcolonial pedagogy, and the support of other teachers such as Meg, who have already developed new teaching units and resources and who are comfortable with an interactive teaching style. In the year after our collaborative study, many other English teachers in Meg's school began to follow her lead in teaching texts outside the traditional canon, offering students choices in novel selection and in ways they could choose to respond to the literature. Meg is now the English department head of a larger urban school and is continuing to make changes in text selection and teaching strategies and to support other staff members to do the same. She has been encouraged by the positive feedback she continues to receive from other teachers, from current and former students, and from a number of immigrant parents. Meg and I have spoken at conferences and workshops together about our work and have formed a reading group of teachers from five different city schools who meet monthly to read and discuss postcolonial literature.

These developments are encouraging, but as both Meg and I discovered from participating in this study, a postcolonial pedagogy involves far more than merely adding a text or two by an African-American, a Puerto Rican, or a Chinese-Canadian writer to an existing curriculum. It demands a commitment to helping students to cross borders constructed within discourses of race, class, gender, and ethnicity so that they can begin to create what Giroux (1992b) describes as "new identities within existing configurations of power" (28). In the process, teachers may find themselves confronted with increasing tensions in the class as students begin to acknowledge their own implications in the relations of power or actively to resist such knowledge. Teachers need to understand that in foregrounding issues such as race and gender in the English classroom, they may have to pay attention to students like Myka, whose reading of *Obasan* unleashed his anger and resentment of Japanese-Canadians, as well as to those like Andrea, whose reading of "Country Lovers" increased her anger at hearing her father talk about "stupid niggers." When teachers engage in a pedagogy that confronts issues of social change and social control, they will need to deal with uncomfortable responses such as these.

In many traditional English classes, where literature is read more for its artistic and literary techniques than for its sociopolitical context, discussion is likely to revolve around questions of symbolism, foreshadowing, and imagery, and around themes such as self-identity, nature, death, or love. The themes of history, described by Mukherjee (1988) as "conquest and subjugation, anti-colonial struggles, racism, sexism, class conflict" (2) are generally absent from this worldview. Mukherjee contends that the tradition of a New Critical approach to teaching texts has encouraged students to totally "disregard local realities" (24) in literature in favor of an emphasis on apolitical, objective, aesthetic readings of texts and a search for universal truths, which are supposed "to speak to all times and all people" (26). Such an approach, she believes, conflicts with a teacher's attempts to introduce a postcolonial reading of literary texts.

Mukherjee's argument highlights an ongoing dilemma for English teachers willing to engage students in a postcolonial pedagogy: how to balance an aesthetic reading of literature with sociopolitical discussions that help students to deconstruct a text's ideology and to question misrepresentations or Eurocentric assumptions. In our study, Meg and I attempted to engage students in both kinds of reading, encouraging them to respond emotionally and personally with a literary text, but also to step back and consider literary elements of the text and to participate in a sociopolitical reading of the literature. Naturally, some texts lent themselves more readily to these multiple readings. Despite our focus on social and political aspects of the texts in our study, we were also anxious to select texts with what we considered to be "aesthetic merit." We were inevitably drawn toward internationally acclaimed writers such as Gabriel García Márquez, Nadine Gordimer, Amy Tan, Rosario Ferré, Zhang Jie, and Yukio Mishima. We discovered that issues of translation add an unanticipated layer of complexity to questions of aesthetics. Some literature, such as the stories by García Márquez, Ferré, and Mishima, read aloud smoothly and poetically in translation, whereas others, such as the Zhang Jie text, seemed somewhat stilted and awkward in our translated version. Questions of translation will continue to be an area of concern in cross-cultural literary studies.

In one grade 12 class, Meg and I encountered another unexpected question about aesthetic quality related to a reading of Nadine Gordimer's poignant story "Happy Event." In a personal interview, Karen, an immigrant student from Vietnam, after explaining that she had been very moved by Gordimer's story of unequal justice for a white woman and her black servant in apartheid South Africa, commented that she would like to read a story by a black South African writer. I remembered that I had read an anthologized story with an unforgettable title, "The Toilet," written by Gcina Mhlope. I considered that this text might offer an interesting comparison to Gordimer's as it describes a struggling black South African writer who is illegally living with her sister in the "servant's quarters" of a rich white woman's home. Meg agreed to introduce the text to the class. Unfortunately, Mhlope's autobiographical short story suffered from being contrasted with the eloquence and complex structure of Gordimer's short story. Students had little to say about the new text and sat in embarrassed silence as Meg explained that she had chosen this story because it was written by a black South African writer. We decided that despite their similar contexts, Mhlope's story was not a good parallel to Gordimer's. This incident raises interesting questions related both to teaching strategies and to aesthetic judgments of non-Western texts. To what degree were students' responses to Mhlope's story influenced by the way we introduced it to them as an "add-on" to Gordimer's? Would they have responded more positively if this story had been read first? More importantly, to what extent did Meg and I attempt to subsume this African text into a pedagogical discourse with monocultural presumptions of aesthetic values?

This teaching moment has increased our interest and concern about what Edward Said has bluntly called "good books and less good books" (in Ryle 1994, 23). We are back into familiar canonical arguments about whether aesthetic judgments are transcultural or culturally relative. Critics have approached this concern in various ways. Ryle (1994), for example, points out that this "value question" is addressed differently in English literary studies, which has based its discipline on the ground of the aesthetic, than in cultural studies, where selection is determined more by the cultural-historical interest of texts than by aesthetic criteria (22). In our study, Meg and I found that we were able to select texts that met both our aesthetic and sociopolitical criteria. Texts that interested us because of their implications in cultural and discursive history were often also good in terms of a more "aesthetic" valuation, described by Ryle as "narrative organisation, descriptive density and precision, vigour of language and so on" (23). We discovered that students can be helped to become aware of and to take pleasure in a work's aesthetic qualities, to consider both the form and the content of the text itself, and to question how the text relates to the broader questions of social implications and constructions that interest us in postcolonial studies. This dual focus allows them to engage on first reading with Coleridge's "willing suspension of disbelief" through a form of humanistic identification and engagement with a text, and then to read more critically, attempting to deconstruct representations of self, place, and other in the text, to contest the authority of the narrative voice, and to specify discourses and sociopractices in which the text is embedded.

This study did not, however, adequately address concerns raised by critics such as the Native American writer Paula Gunn Allen, who argues that texts arising from an oral tradition have their own forms, narrative structures, and allusive systems and should not be considered using aesthetic criteria arising from a Western literary tradition. Gunn Allen (1995) suggests that "no cultural artifact can be seen as existing outside its particular matrix; no document, however profoundly aesthetic, can be comprehended outside its frame of reference….Because Western societies are fundamentally the same…Eurocentric critics think that culture is a unified field" (36–37). Similarly, David Palumbo-Liu (1995) argues that postcolonial texts are added to the canon only after efforts to neutralize their historical and political contradictions and differences. He cautions that the insertion of ethnicity into the curriculum can be articulated through pedagogical discourses that ultimately defer to monocultural presumptions of "aesthetic value," "expressive force," "character formation," and the ethnic text reduced to a pretext for the pluralistic argument that all cultures share certain expressive values (2).

These concerns will need to be considered in future studies that address teachers' questions about how to make aesthetic judgments about non-Western literature and how to introduce the texts to students in ways that explore their tensions and contradictory demands.

This study has attempted to understand how postcolonial literary texts can challenge readers in contemporary classrooms to begin revisioning and re-mapping the world, helping them to cross cultural and political borders. As the Japanese-American writer Kyoko Mori (1995) discovered when she was sitting in the Tokyo airport after spending eight weeks revisiting Japan, the way we look at the world and our connection to the world depends on our particular viewpoint. A map of the world looks quite different from a new vantage point:

> On the wall behind some of the benches, there is a map of the five continents advertising an airline. Somehow, the map looks slightly skewed or wrong, until I realize that it doesn't have the United States at the center, like the maps I have been looking at in the last thirteen years. This is the map of my childhood, with Tokyo at its center. From that center, lines, indicating regularly scheduled flights, run all over the world, thin as webwork, blue and red like bloodlines diagrammed in schoolbooks. (275)

Many of our students from minority backgrounds in today's classrooms are accustomed to looking at a map of the world from diverse and often contradictory viewpoints. Most of our students from mainstream backgrounds have been accustomed to seeing themselves at the center of the world map, a viewpoint reinforced by their readings of Western canonized literary texts. For all these students, reading literature in the context of a postcolonial pedagogy can offer possibilities to engage more thoughtfully in diverse and pluralistic human adventures. Anne Michaels, in her novel *Fugitive Pieces* (1996), reflects on the Catalan Atlas, the definitive map of its time, which included the latest information brought back by Arabic and European travelers. Instead of labeling unknown northern and southern regions of the world as places of myth, monsters, and sea serpents as other maps of the time did, this truth-seeking atlas simply left these frighteningly unknown parts of the world blank and labeled them "Terra Incognita." As Michaels (1996) writes,

> Maps of history have always been less honest. Terra Cognita and Terra Incognita inhabit exactly the same coordinates of time and space. The closest we come to knowing the location of what's unknown is when it melts through the map like a watermark, a stain as transparent as a drop of rain. (136–37)

For contemporary students in our classrooms, much of the world is still this terrifying Terra Incognita, inhabited with the myths and monsters of their imagination. The challenge for the future will be to find ways to encourage teachers to introduce a postcolonial pedagogy that will begin to dispel the myths.

Appendices

Text Selections for Grade 10 Classes

Short Stories
From Rochman, Hazel, ed. 1988. *Somehow Tenderness Survives: Stories of Southern Africa*. New York: HarperKeypoint.
Nadine Gordimer (*South Africa*). "Country Lovers."

From Barry, James, ed. 1992. *The Storyteller: Short Stories from Around the World*. Scarborough, Ont.: Nelson Canada.
Yukio Mishima (Trans. Ivan Morris) (*Japan*). "Swaddling Clothes."
Vilas Manivat (Trans. Jennifer Draskau) (*Thailand*). "Who Needs It?"
Yu-Wol Chong-Nyon (Trans. Chong-Nyon & Daniel L. Milton) (*Korea*). "The Non-revolutionaries."
Zhang Jie (Trans. Gladys Yang) (*China*). "Love Must Not Be Forgotten."

Poetry
From Wowk, Jerry and Ted Jason, eds. 1993. *Multiculturalism: The Issues Collection*.
Bert Almon (*Canada*). "Heritage Days."
Nigel Darbasie (*Canada*). "Our Subdivision."
Jim Wong-Chu (*Canada*). "Equal Opportunity."
Maya Angelou (*United States*). "And Still I Rise."

Essay
From Wowk, Jerry and Ted Jason, eds. 1993. *Multiculturalism: The Issues Collection*.
Gerry Weiner (*Canada*). "Youth Our Best Hope to End Racial Discrimination."

Novels
Harper Lee (*United States*). *To Kill a Mockingbird* (class study).

Small-group novel study with choice among four novels:
Mildred Taylor (*United States*). *The Road to Memphis*.

Lyll Becerra de Jenkins (*Colombia/United States*). *The Honorable Prison.*
William Bell (*Canada*). *Forbidden City.*
Suzanne Fisher Staples (*United States*). *Shabanu, Daughter of the Wind.*

Film
Cry Freedom

Drama
William Shakespeare, *Romeo and Juliet* (students chose between this play and *Julius Caesar*).
Frederick Knott, *Wait Until Dark* (this play was selected because of the city stage production).

Text Selections for Grade 11 Advanced Placement (AP) Class

Short Stories
From Rosen, Gayle, Marilyn Chapman and Lesley Elliott, eds. 1991. *The Story Begins When the Story Ends: Canadian and World Short Fiction.* Scarborough, Ont.: Prentice-Hall Canada.
V.S. Naipaul (*Trinidad/Britain*). "B. Wordsworth."
Abioseh Nicol (*Sierra Leone*). "The Judge's Son."
Nadine Gordimer (*South Africa*). "Another Part of the Sky."

From Iveson, M., J.E. Oster, and J. McClay, eds. 1990. *Literary Experiences Volume 1.* Scarborough, Ont.: Prentice-Hall Canada.
Henry Kreisel (*Canada*). "The Broken Globe."

Poetry
From Iveson, M., J.E. Oster, and J. McClay, eds. 1990. *Literary Experiences Vol. One.* Scarborough, Ont.: Prentice-Hall Canada.
Michael Ondaatje (*Canada*). "To a Sad Daughter."
Atukwei Okai (*Ghana*). "999 Smiles."
Joy Kogawa (*Canada*). "Woodtick" (and other Kogawa poetry).
Selected poems from *Multicultural Perspectives.* Applebee, Arthur N. and Judith Langer, eds. 1993. Evanston, Il: McDougall, Littell.

Novels
Joy Kogawa (*Canada*). *Obasan.*

Individual choice of novel for book talks.

Novel/Non Fiction
Variety of Canadian essays by Margaret Laurence and others.
Variety of articles linked with short stories.

Drama
William Shakespeare, *Macbeth* (students voted on which Shakespeare play to read).
Tennessee Williams, *The Glass Menagerie.*

Preliminary Literary Selections for Possible Inclusion in the Grade 12 Curriculum

In *New Worlds of Literature.* 1989. Eds. Jerome Beaty and Paul J. Hunter. New York: W.W. Norton.
Blaise Clark. "A Class of New Canadians." Short story, 960–67.
Maxine Hong Kingston: "No Name Woman." Chapter 1 of *The Woman Warrior,* 299–308.
Michael Ondaatje. "Light." Poem, 312–14.
Gabrielle Roy. "Wilhelm." Short story, 793–98.

In *Multicultural Perspectives.* 1993. Eds. Arthur N. Applebee and Judith Langer. Evanston, Il: McDougall, Littell.
Diana Chang. "Saying Yes." Poem, 209.
Gabriel García Márquez. "A Very Old Man with Enormous Wings." Short story, 266–73.
Frank Marschall Davis. "Tenement Room: Chicago." Poem, 288.
Mark Mathabane. Excerpt from *Kaffir Boy,* 222–31.
Pablo Neruda. "Ode to the Watermelon." Trans. Robert Bly. Poem, 302–04.
Richard Rodriguez. Excerpt from *Hunger of Memory,* 169–72.
Wendy Rose. "Loo–Wit." Poem, 290.
Amy Tan. "Two Kinds." Excerpt from *The Joy Luck Club,* 198–205.

In *Literary Experiences Vol. Two.* 1989. Eds. M. Iveson, J.E. Oster and J. McClay. Scarborough, Ont.: Prentice-Hall Canada.
Julia de Burgos. "Julia de Burgos." Trans. G. Shulman. Poem, 414–15.
Janet Frame. "A Boy's Will." Short Story, 133–44.
Gail Godwin. "A Cultural Exchange." Short story, 224–42.
A.L. Hendricks. "Jamaican Fragment." Short story, 362–64.
Langston Hughes. "As I Grew Older." Poem, 469.

Tillie Olsen. "I Stand Here Ironing." Short story, 405–13.
Santha Rama Rau. "Return to India." Essay, 337–47.
Richard Rodriguez. "Complexion." Short story, 416–36.
Gabrielle Roy. "The Dead Child." Trans. J. Marshall. Short story, 218–23.

In *An Anthology of Canadian Native Literature in English.* 1992. Eds. Daniel David Moses and Terry Goldie. Toronto: Oxford University Press.
Armand Garnet Ruffo. "Archie Belaney, 1930–31." Poem, 319–20.
Rita Joe. "Today's Learning Child." Poem, 113.
Basil Johnson. "Is That All There Is? Tribal Literature." Essay, 105–12.

In *The Story Begins Where the Story Ends: Canadian and World Short Fiction.* 1991. Eds. Gayle Rosen, Marilyn Chapman and Lesley Elliott. Scarborough, Ont.: Prentice-Hall Canada.
V.S. Naipaul. "B. Wordsworth." Short story, 79–85.

In *The Eye of the Heart: Short Stories from Latin America.* 1973. Ed. Barbara Howes. New York: Avon.
Mario Vargas Llosa. "Sunday, Sunday." Trans. Alastair Reid. Short story, 535–55.

In *Imaginary Homelands: Essays and Criticism 1981–1991.* 1991. Salman Rushdie. London: Granta Books.
Salman Rushdie. "Censorship." Essay, 37–40.

Final Text Selections for Grade 12

Short Stories and Essays
From Iveson, M., J.E. Oster, J. McClay, eds. 1990. *Literary Experiences Vol. Two.* Scarborough, Ont.: Prentice-Hall, Canada.
Nadine Gordimer (*South Africa*). "Happy Event" (short story).
Margaret Laurence (*Canada*). "Where the World Began" (essay).
Santha Rama Rau (*India*). "Return to India" (essay).

From *Multicultural Perspectives.* Applebee, Arthur N. and Judith Lange, eds. 1993. Evanston, Il: McDougall, Littell.
Rosario Ferré (*Puerto Rico*). "The Youngest Doll" (short story).
Gabriel García Márquez (*Colombia*). "A Very Old Man with Enormous Wings" (short story).

Amy Tan (*United States*). "Two Kinds" (from *The Joy Luck Club*).

From Stephenson, Craig, ed. 1993. *Countries of Invention: Contemporary World Writing*. Toronto Ont.: Addison-Wesley and Rubicon.
Amy Tan (*United States*). "Mother Tongue" (essay).

Poetry
From Iveson, M, J.E. Oster, and J. McClay, eds. 1990. *Literary Experiences Vol. Two*.
Carl Leggo (Canada). "Tangled."

From Applebee, Arthur N. and Judith Lange, eds. 1993. *Multicultural Perspectives*
Diana Chang (United States). "Saying Yes."
Variety of poetry from *Multicultural Perspectives, Literary Experiences*, and other anthologies—Canadian and international.

Drama
Peter Schaffer, *Royal Hunt of the Sun*.
William Shakespeare, *Hamlet/Othello* (students chose one).

Novel/Nonfiction
Students chose a novel and nonfiction title from a list of possible titles for book talks.

References

Achebe, Chinua. 1978. "An Image of Africa." *Research into African Literatures* 9: 12.

Alladin, Ibrahim. 1992. "Multicultural Education in Canada: Rhetoric and Reality." *Education and Society* 10, no. 2: 73–82.

Altmann, Anna; Ingrid Johnston; and Margaret Mackey. 1998. "Curriculum Decisions about Literature in Contemporary Classrooms: A Preliminary Analysis of a Survey of Materials Used in Edmonton Grade 10 Classes." *The Alberta Journal of Educational Research* XLIV, no. 2: 208–20.

Apple, Michael W. 1993. *Official Knowledge: Democratic Education in a Conservative Age.* New York: Routledge.

Applebee, Arthur N. 1993. *Literature in the Secondary School.* Research Report No. 25. Urbana, Illinois: NCTE.

———. 1990. *A Study of High School Literature Anthologies.* Report 1.5. New York: Center for the Learning and Teaching of Literature.

———. 1989. *A Study of Book-Length Works Taught in High-School English Courses.* Report 1.2. New York: Center for the Learning and Teaching of Literature.

Applebee, Arthur N. and Judith Langer. 1993. *Multicultural Experiences.* Evanston, Il: McDougal, Littell.

Arnold, Matthew. [1869] 1981. *Culture and Anarchy.* London: Smith, Elder.

Aronowitz, Stanley and Henry Giroux. 1991. *Postmodern Education: Politics, Culture and Social Criticism.* Minneapolis: Univ. of Minnesota Press.

Ashcroft, Bill. 2001. *Post-Colonial Transformations.* London: Routledge.

Ashcroft, Bill; Gareth Griffiths; and Helen Tiffin. 1989. *The Empire Writes Back: Theory and Practice in Post-Colonial Literatures.* London: Routledge.

Atwood, Margaret. 1972. *Survival: A Thematic Guide to Canadian Literature.* Toronto: Anansi.

Bahri, Deepika. 1995. "Once More with Feeling: What Is Postcolonialism?" *Ariel: A Review of International English Literature* 26, no. 1: 51–82.

Bakhtin, Mikhail. 1984. *Problems of Dostoevsky's Poetics.* Trans. Caryl Emerson. Minneapolis: Univ. of Minnesota Press.

———. 1981. *The Dialogic Imagination.* Eds. and trans. Michael Holquist and Caryl Emerson. Austin: Univ. of Texas Press.

Baldwin, James. 1955. *Notes of a Native Son*. New York: Beacon Press.

Bannerji, Himani. 1995. *Thinking Through: Essays on Feminism, Marxism, and Anti-Racism*. Toronto: Women's Press.

Barthes, Roland. 1982. *Camera Lucida: Reflections on Photography*. New York: Noonday Press.

———. 1978. *The Pleasures of the Text*. New York: Hill and Wang.

———. 1977. "The Rhetoric of the Image." In *Image/Music/Text*, ed. and trans. Stephen Heath, 32–51. New York: Noonday Press.

Behdad, Ali. 1993. "Travelling to Teach: Postcolonial Critics in the American Academy." In *Race, Identity and Representation in Education*, eds. Cameron McCarthy and Warren Crichlow, 40–49. New York: Routledge.

Bhabha, Homi K. 1996. "Unpacking my Library...Again." In *The Post-Colonial Question*, eds. Iain Chambers and Lidia Curti, 199–211. New York: Routledge.

———. 1994. *The Location of Culture*. London: Routledge.

———. 1990. *Nation and Narration*. London: Routledge.

———. 1986. "Foreword" to Franz Fanon, *Black Skin, White Masks*. London: Pluto Press.

Birkerts, Sven. 1994. *The Gutenberg Elegies: The Fate of Reading in an Electronic Age*. Boston: Faber and Faber.

Bissoondath, Neil. 1994. *Selling Illusions: The Cult of Multiculturalism in Canada*. Toronto: Penguin.

———. 1993. *The Globe and Mail*. January 28, A17.

Bloom, Alan. 1987. *The Closing of the American Mind: How Higher Education Has Failed Democracy and Impoverished the Souls of Today's Students*. New York: Simon and Schuster.

Bloom, Harold. 1994. *The Western Canon: The Books and School of the Ages*. New York: Riverhead Books.

Brand, Dionne. 2001. *A Map to the Door of No Return: Notes to Belonging*. Toronto: Doubleday Canada.

Britzman, Deborah P. 1991. "Decentering Discourses in Teacher Education: Or, the Unleashing of Unpopular Things." *Boston University Journal of Education* 173, no. 3: 60–80.

Britzman, Deborah P.; Kelvin A. Santiago-Valles; Gladys M. Jiménez-Muñoz; and Laura Lamash. 1993. "Slips That Show and Tell: Fashioning Multiculture as a Problem of Representation." In *Race, Identity and Representation in Education*, eds. Cameron McCarthy and Warren Crichlow, 188–200. New York: Routledge.

Bruner, Jerome. 1990. *Acts of Meaning*. Cambridge: Harvard University Press.

Buchan, John. [1910] 1938. *Prester John.* Boston: Houghton Mifflin Company.

Burton, Robert S. 1992. "Talking Across Cultures." In *Understanding Others: Cultural and Cross-Cultural Studies and the Teaching of Literature,* eds. Joseph Trimmer and Tilly Warnock, 115–23. Urbana, Il: NCTE.

Cameron, Robert B. 1989. *A Study of the Current Implementation of Canadian Literature in Alberta High Schools.* Ph.D. diss., University of Alberta.

Chambers, Iain. 1994a. *Migrancy Culture Identity.* London: Routledge.

———. 1994b. "Leaky Habits and Broken Grammar." In *Travellers' Tales,* eds. George Robertson et al., 245–49. London: Routledge.

Clifford, James. 1992. "Traveling Cultures." In *Cultural Studies,* eds. Lawrence Grossberg, Cary Nelson, and Paula A. Treichler, 96–116. New York: Routledge.

Connelly, Michael F. and Jean D. Clandinin. 1988. *Teachers as Curriculum Planners: Narratives of Experience.* New York: Teachers College Press.

Cox, Brian. 1992. "English Studies and National Identity." In *Reassessing Language and Literacy,* eds. Mike Hayhoe and Stephen Parker, 1–10. Buckingham, England: Open University Press.

Dasenbrock, Reed Way. 1992. "Teaching Multicultural Literature." In *Understanding Others: Cultural and Cross-Cultural Studies and the Teaching of Literature,* eds. Joseph Trimmer and Tilly Warnock, 35–46. Urbana, Il: NCTE.

Deleuze, Gilles and Felix Guattari. 1987. *A Thousand Plateaus: Capitalism and Schizophrenia.* Trans. B. Massumi. Minneapolis: Univ. of Minnesota Press.

Derrida, Jacques. 1978. *Writing and Difference.* Trans. A. Bass. Chicago: Univ. of Chicago Press.

Diamond, C.T. Patrick. 1995. "Education and the Narrative of Self: Of Maps and Stories." *Advances in Personal Construct Psychology* 3: 79–100.

Dias, Patrick. 1992a. "Literary Reading and Classroom Constraints: Aligning Practice with Theory." In *Literature Instruction: A Focus on Student Response,* ed. Judith A. Langer, 131–62. Urbana, Il: NCTE.

———. 1992b. "Cultural Literacy, National Curriculum: What (and *How*) Does Every Canadian Student Really Need to Know?" *English Quarterly* 24: 3–4, 10–19.

Dimic, Milan, V. 1988. "Models and Paradigms for the Study of Canadian Literature: Its Internal and External Relations as Perceived by Critics and Scholars—a Comparatist View." *Problems of Literary Perceptions/Problèmes de Reception Litteraire,* eds. E.D. Blodgett and A.G. Purdy, 144–67. Edmonton: Univ. of Alberta Press.

Dirlik, Arif. 1994. "The Postcolonial Aura: Third World Criticism in the Age of Global Capitalism." *Critical Inquiry* 20: 328–56.

Dollimore, Jonathan. 1984. "Beyond Essentialist Humanism." In *Issues in Contemporary Literary Theory,* ed. Peter Barry, 38–52. London: Macmillan Education.

Duncan, James and David Ley, eds. 1993. *Place/Culture/Representation.* London, England: Routledge.

Eaglestone, Robert. 2000. *Doing English: A Guide for Literature Students.* London: Routledge.

Eagleton, Terry. 1983. *Literary Theory: An Introduction.* Oxford: Basil Blackwell.

Eco, Umberto. 1994. *Six Walks in the Fictional Woods.* Cambridge: Harvard University Press.

Eisner, Elliot. 1988. "The Primacy of Experience and the Politics of Method." *Educational Researcher* 17, no. 5: 15–20.

"English for Ages 5 to 16." 1989. *The Cox Report.* London: HMSO.

Fanon, Franz. 1963. *The Wretched of the Earth.* London: Pluto Press.

Ferré, Rosario. 1993. "The Youngest Doll." In *Multicultural Perspectives,* eds. Arthur N. Applebee and Judith Langer, 274–80. Evanston, Il: McDougal, Littell.

Fleras, Augie and Jean Leonard Elliot. 1992. *The Challenge of Diversity: Multiculturalism in Canada.* Scarborough, Ont.: Nelson.

Freire, Paulo. 1970. *Pedagogy of the Oppressed.* New York: Continuum.

Gabriel, John. 1994. *Racism Culture Markets.* London: Routledge.

Galloway, Priscilla. 1980. *What's Wrong with High-School English? It's Sexist...Un-Canadian...Outdated.* Toronto: OISE.

García Márquez, Gabriel. 1993. "A Very Old Man with Enormous Wings." In *Multicultural Perspectives,* eds. Arthur N. Applebee and Judith Langer, 266–73. Evanston, Il: McDougal, Littell.

Gilbert, Pam. 1983. "Down among the Women: Girls as Readers and Writers." *English in Australia* 64: 26–9.

Giroux, Henry A. 1992a. "Liberal Education and the Struggle for Public Life: Dreaming about Democracy." In *The Politics of Liberal Education,* eds. Darryl L. Gless and Barbara Herrnstein, 119–44. Durham, N.C.: Duke University Press.

————. 1992b. *Border Crossings: Cultural Workers and the Politics of Education.* New York: Routledge.

————. 1988. *Schooling and the Struggle for Public Life: Critical Pedagogy in the Modern Age.* Minneapolis: Univ. of Minnesota Press.

Goebel, Bruce A. and James C. Hall, eds. 1995. *Teaching a "New Canon"? Students, Teachers, and Texts in the College Literature Classroom.* Urbana, Il: NCTE.

Goldberg, David Theo. 1993. *Racist Culture: Philosophy and the Politics of Meaning.* Oxford, England: Blackwell.

Goody, Joan and Hugh Knight. 1985. "Multi-Cultural Education and Anti-Racist Teaching." *English in Education* 19, no. 3: 3–7.

Gorak, Jan. 1991. *The Making of the Modern Canon.* London: Athlone.

Gordimer, Nadine. 1995. *Writing and Being.* Cambridge: Harvard University Press.

————.1990. "Happy Event." In *Literary Experiences Vol. Two,* eds. Margaret Iveson, John Oster and Jill McClay, 348–61. Scarborough, Ont.: Prentice-Hall Canada.

Graff, Gerald. 1996. "Organizing the Conflicts in the Curriculum." In *Critical Theory and the Teaching of Literature,* eds. J. F. Slevin and A. Young, 125–139. Urbana, Il: NCTE.

————. 1992. *Beyond the Culture Wars: How Teaching the Conflicts Can Revitalize American Education.* New York: Routledge.

————. 1990. "Teach the Conflicts." *South Atlantic Quarterly* 89, no. 1: 51–67.

Greene, Maxine. 1995. "Multiple Voices and Multiple Realities." *Releasing the Imagination.* San Francisco: Jossey-Bass.

————. 1993. "The Passions of Pluralism: Multiculturalism and the Expanding Community." *Educational Researcher* 55:1, 13–18.

Greenlaw, James C. 1994. *A Postcolonial Conception of the High School Multicultural Literature Curriculum.* Ph.D. diss., University of British Columbia.

Grumet, Madeleine. 1988. *Bittermilk: Women and Teaching.* Amherst: University of Massachussetts Press.

Guillén, Claudio. 1993. *The Challenge of Comparative Literature.* Trans. Cola Franzen. Cambridge: Harvard University Press.

Gunn Allen, Paula. 1995. "'Border Studies': The Intersection of Gender and Color." In *The Ethnic Canon,* ed. David Palumbo-Liu, 31–47. Minneapolis: Univ. of Minnesota Press.

Hall, Catherine. 1996. "Histories, Empires and the Post-Colonial Moment." In *The Post-Colonial Question,* eds. Iain Chambers and Lidia Curti, 65–77. London: Routledge.

Hall, James C. 1995. "Towards the Success of a 'New Canon': Radical Introspection as Critical Practice." In *Teaching a "New Canon"? Students, Teachers, and Texts in the College Literature Classroom,* eds. Bruce A. Goebel and James C. Hall, 3–21. Urbana, Il: NCTE.

Hall, Stuart. 1991. "Teaching Race." In *The School in the Multicultural Society,* eds. A. James and R. Jeffcoate, 58–69. London: Harper & Row.

Hansson, Gunnar. 1992. "Readers Responding—and Then?" *Research in the Teaching of English* 26: 2, 135–48.

Harley, J. Brian. 1988. "Maps, Knowledge and Power." In *The Iconography of Landscape: Essays on the Symbolic Representation, Design and Use of Past Environments.* Cambridge, England: Cambridge University Press.

Hayles, Katherine. 1989. "Chaos as Orderly Disorder: Shifting Ground in Contemporary Literature and Science." *New Literary History* 20: 305–19.

Heaney, Seamus. 1995. *The Redress of Poetry.* London: Faber and Faber.

Herrnstein-Smith, Barbara. 1984. "Contingencies of Value." In *Canons,* ed. Robert von Halleberg, 7–8. Chicago: University of Chicago Press.

Hirsch, E.D. Jr. 1987. *Cultural Literacy: What Every American Needs to Know.* New York: Houghton Mifflin.

hooks, bell. 1994. *Teaching to Transgress: Education as the Practice of Freedom.* New York: Routledge.

———. 1992. *Yearning: Race, Gender and Cultural Politics.* Toronto: Between the Lines.

———. 1991. "Narratives of Struggle." In *Critical Fictions,* ed. Philomena Mariana, 53–61. Seattle, Wash.: Bay Press.

Hutcheon, Linda. 1995. "Circling the Downspout of Empire: Postcolonialism and Postmodernism." In *The Post-Colonial Studies Reader,* eds. Bill Ashcroft, Gareth Griffiths, and Helen Tiffin, 130–35. London: Routledge.

Hutcheon, Linda and Marion Richmond, eds. 1990. *Other Solitudes: Canadian Multicultural Fictions.* Toronto: Oxford University Press.

"An Inquiry into the Education of Children from Ethnic Minority Groups." 1985. *The Swann Report.* London: HMSO.

Iser, Wolfgang. 1987. "The Reading Process." In *Issues in Contemporary Critical Theory,* ed. Peter Barry, 105–19. London: Macmillan Education.

———. 1978. *The Act of Reading: A Theory of Aesthetic Response.* Baltimore: John Hopkins University Press.

Iveson, Margaret, John Oster, and Jill McClay, eds. 1990. *Literary Experiences Vol. Two*. Scarborough, Ont.: Prentice-Hall Canada.

———. 1989. *Literary Experiences Vol. One*. Scarborough, Ont.: Prentice-Hall Canada.

Janks, Hilary and Jonathan Paton. 1990. "English and the Teaching of English Literature in South Africa." In *Teaching and Learning English Worldwide*, eds. James Britton et al. 226–48. Clevedon, United Kingdom: Multilingual Matters.

Johnston, Ingrid. 1996. "Point of View in Literary Texts: A Perspective on Unexamined Racist Ideologies in the High School English Curriculum." In *Racism in Canadian Schools*, ed. M. Ibrahim Alladin, 107–119. Toronto: Harcourt Brace.

———. 1994. "Shared Teaching of Multicultural Literature: A Researcher's Perceptions." *English Quarterly* 26: 4, 27–32.

Johnston, Ingrid and Jyoti Mangat. 2002. "Making the Invisible Visible: Stereotypes of Masculinities in Canonized High School Texts." In *Ways of Being Male: Representing Masculinities in Children's Literature and Film*, ed. John Stephens, 133–49. New York: Routledge.

Jusdanis, Gregory. 1991. *Belated Modernity and Aesthetic Culture: Inventing National Literature*. Minneapolis: Univ. of Minnesota Press.

Kincaid, Jamaica. 1988. *A Small Place*. New York: Plume.

Kogawa, Joy. 1992. *Itsuka*. New York: Viking.

———. 1983. *Obasan*. Markham, Ont.: Penguin Books.

Krupat, Arnold. 1992. *Ethnocriticism: Ethnography, History, Literature*. Berkeley: University of California Press.

Laiwan. 1992. "The Imperialism of Syntax." In *Many-Mouthed Birds: Contemporary Writing by Chinese-Canadians*, eds. Bennett Lee and Jim Wong-Chu, 57. Vancouver B.C.: Douglas and McIntyre.

Landow, George P. 1992. *Hypertext*. Baltimore: The Johns Hopkins University Press.

Lanier, Douglas. 1991. "Less Is More: Coverage, Critical Diversity, and the Limits of Pluralism." In *Practicing Theory in Introductory College Literature Courses*, eds. James M. Calahan and David B. Downing, 199–212. Urbana, Il: NCTE.

Laurence, Margaret. 1990. "Where the World Began." In *Literary Experiences, Vol. Two*, eds. Margaret Iveson, John Oster, and Jill McClay, 252–57. Scarborough, Ont.: Prentice-Hall Canada.

Leavis, F.R. 1930. *Mass Civilisation and Minority Culture*. Cambridge, England: Gordon Fraser.

Lee, Bennett, Jim Wong-Chu (1991) *Many-Mouthed Birds: Contemporary Writing by Chinese Canadians* Seattle: Univ. of Washington Press

Leggo, Carl. 1990. "Tangled." In *Literary Experiences, Vol. Two,* eds. Margaret Iveson, John Oster, and Jill McClay, 250–51. Scarborough, Ont.: Prentice-Hall Canada.

Lorde, Audre. 1988. *Charting the Journey: Writings by Black and Third World Women.* London: Sheba Feminist Publishers.

Lynch, James. 1986. *Multicultural Education: Principles and Practice.* London: Routledge and Kegan Paul.

Mackey, Margaret. 1995. *Imagining with Words: The Temporal Processes of Reading Fiction.* Ph.D. diss., University of Alberta.

McCarthy, Cameron. 1993. "After the Canon: Knowledge and Ideological Representation in the Multicultural Discourse on Curriculum Reform." In *Race, Identity and Representation in Education,* eds. Cameron McCarthy and Warren Crichlow, 289–305. New York: Routledge.

McCarthy, Cameron and Warren Crichlow, eds. 1993. *Race, Identity and Representation in Education.* New York: Routledge.

McLaren. Peter. 1993/1992. "Critical Literacy and Postcolonial Praxis: A Freirian Perspective." *College Literature,* Double Issue, 19.3/20.1: 7–27.

McLeod. John. 2000. *Beginning Postcolonialism.* Manchester, England: Manchester University Press.

Michaels, Anne. 1996. *Fugitive Pieces.* Toronto: McClelland Stewart.

Minh-ha, Trinh T. 1994. "Other Than Myself/My Other Self." In *Travellers' Tales: Narratives of Home and Displacement,* eds. George Robertson, Melinda Mash, Lisa Tickner, Jon Bird, and Barry Curtix. 9–26. London: Routledge.

Mistry, Rohinton. 2002. *Family Matters.* Toronto: McClelland and Stewart.

Mizell, Linda; Susan Benett; Bisse Bowman; and Laraine Morin. 1993. "Different Ways of Seeing: Teaching in an Anti-Racist School." In *Freedom's Plow,* eds. Theresa Perry and James W. Fraser, 27–46. New York: Routledge.

Mori, Kyoko. 1995. *The Dream of Water.* New York: Fawcett Columbine.

Morrison, Toni. 1989. "Unspeakable Things Unspoken: The Afro-American Presence in American Literature." In *Michigan Quarterly Review,* ed. Laurence Goldstein, Winter: 1–34.

———. 1987. *Beloved.* New York: Plume.

Mukherjee, Arun. 1998. *Postcolonialism: My Living.* Toronto. Ont.: TSAR.

———. 1988. *Towards an Aesthetic of Opposition: Essays on Literature Criticism and Cultural Imperialism.* Toronto: Williams-Wallace.

Naidoo, Beverley. 1992. *Through Whose Eyes? Exploring Racism: Reader, Text and Context.* Stoke-on-Trent, Staff., England: Trentham Books.

Ndebele, Njabulo S. 1994. *South African Literature and Culture.* Manchester, England: Manchester University Press.

Palumbo-Liu, David. 1995. *The Ethnic Canon: History, Institutions, Interventions.* Minneapolis: Univ. of Minnesota Press.

Philip, M. Nourbese. 1992. *Frontiers: Essays and Writings on Racism and Culture.* Stratford, Ont.: The Mercury Press.

Pratt, Mary Louise. 1996. "Daring to Dream: Re-Visioning Culture and Citizenship." In *Critical Theory and the Teaching of Literature,* eds. James F. Slevin and Art Young, 3–20. Urbana, Il: NCTE.

———. 1991. "Arts of the Contact Zone." *Profession* 9, no. 1: 33–40.

Pringle, Thomas. 1946. "The Kaffir." *The New Centenary Book of South African Verse,* ed. Francis Slater, 7. London: Longman.

Quayson, Ato. 2000. *Postcolonialism: Theory, Practice or Process?* Cambridge, England: Polity Press.

Rau, Santha Rama. 1990. "Return to India." In *Literary Experiences, Vol. Two,* eds. Margaret Iveson, John Oster, and Jill McClay, 338–47. Scarborough, Ont.: Prentice-Hall Canada.

"Report of the Committee of Inquiry into the Teaching of English Language." 1988. *The Kingman Report.* London: HMSO.

Rosenblatt, Louise M. 1978. *The Reader, the Text, the Poem: the Transactional Theory of the Literary Work.* Carbondale: Southern Illinois Press.

Rushdie, Salman. [1983] 1992. "'Commonwealth Literature' Does not Exist." In *Imaginary Homelands,* 61–70. London: Penguin.

———. 1990. *Haroun and the Sea of Stories.* London: Granta Books.

———. 1984. *Shame.* London: Picador.

Ryan, Simon. 1994. "Cartography, Exploration, and the Construction of Australia." In *De-scribing Empire,* eds. Chris Tiffin and Alan Lawson, 115–30. London: Routledge.

Ryle, Martin. 1994. "Long Live Literature? Englit, Radical Criticism and Cultural Studies." *Radical Philosophy* 67 (Summer): 21–27.

Said, Edward. 1993. *Culture and Imperialism.* New York: Alfred A. Knopf.

———. 1991. "Identity, Authority, and Freedom: The Potentate and the Traveller." *Transition* 54: 4–18.

———. 1990. "Reflections on Exile." In *Out There, Marginalisation and Contemporary Culture,* eds. Russell Ferguson, Martha Gever, Trinh T. Minh-ha, and Cornel West, 357–363. Cambridge, Mass.: MIT Press.

———. 1978. *Orientalism.* London: Routledge and Kegan Paul.

Samantrai, Ranu. 1995. "States of Belonging: Pluralism, Migrancy, Literature." In *Essays on Canadian Writing* 57: 33–50.

Samson, Anne. 1992. *F.R. Leavis.* New York: Harvester Wheatsheaf.

Scafe, Suzanne. 1989. *Teaching Black Literature.* London: Virago.

Senanu, K.E. and T. Vincent, eds. 1977 (1970). *A Selection of African Poetry (Revised and Enlarged Edition).* Harlow, England: Longman.

Sepamla, Sipho. 1982. "The Black Writer in South Africa Today: Problems
and Dilemmas." In *Soweto Poetry,* ed. Michael Chapman, 116. Johan-
nesburg, South Africa: McGraw-Hill.

Slater, Francis, ed. 1946. *The New Centenary Book of South African Verse.*
London: Longman.

Slemon, Stephen. 1994. "The Scramble for Post-Colonialism." In *De-
scribing Empire,* eds. Chris Tiffin and Alan Lawson, 15–32. London:
Routledge.

Smagorinsky, Peter. 1995. "New Canons, New Problems: The Challenge of
Promoting a Sense of Kinship among Students of Diversity." In *Teaching a "New Canon"?: Students, Teachers, and Texts in the College Literature Classroom,* 48–64. Urbana, Il: NCTE.

———. 1992. "Towards a Civic Education in a Multicultural Society:
Ethical Problems in Teaching Literature." *English Education*: 212–
28.

Spears-Bunton, Linda. 1990. "Welcome to My House: African American
and European American Students' Responses to Virginia Hamilton's
House of Dies Drear." Journal of Negro Education 59, no. 4: 566–575.

Spivak, Gayatri. 1988. "Can the Subaltern Speak?" In *Marxism and the Interpretation of Culture,* eds. Cary Nelson and Lawrence Grossberg,
271–313. Chicago: University of Illinois Press.

Steiner, Wendy. 1995. *The Scandal of Pleasure: Art in an Age of Funda-
mentalism.* Chicago: University of Chicago Press.

Sumara, Dennis. 1994. *The Literary Imagination and the Curriculum.*
Ph.D. diss., University of Alberta.

Tan, Amy. 1993. "Two Kinds." In *Multicultural Perspectives,* eds. Arthur N. Applebee and Judith Langer, 198–208. Evanston, Il: McDougal, Littell.

———. 1993. "Mother Tongue." In *Countries of Invention: Contemporary World Writing,* ed. Craig Stephenson, 278–84. Toronto: Addison-Wesley Publishers.

Taylor, Charles. 1992. *The Malaise of Modernity.* The Massey Lectures
Series. Concord, Ont.: House of Anansi Press.

Taylor, Mildred. 1990. *The Road to Memphis.* New York: Dial Books.

_____. 1976. *Roll of Thunder, Hear My Cry*. New York: Dial Books.

Thomson, Jack. 1992. "The Significance and Uses of Contemporary Literary Theory." In *Reconstructing Literature Teaching: New Essays on the Teaching of Literature*, ed. Jack Thomson, 1–8. Norwood, S.A.: Australian Association for the Teaching of English.

Tompkins, Jane. 1990. "Pedagogy of the Distressed." *College English* 52, no. 6: 653–60.

———. 1980. "The Reader in History: The Changing Shape of Literary Response." In *Reader-Response Criticism: From Formalism to Post-Structuralism*, ed. Jane P. Tompkins, 201–26. Baltimore: John Hopkins University Press.

Tredell, Nicolas. 1987. "Euphoria (Ltd)—The Limitations of Post-Structuralism and Deconstruction." In *Issues in Contemporary Critical Theory*, ed. Peter Barry, 91–104. London: Macmillan Education.

Tymoczko, Maria. 2000. "Translations of Themselves: The Contours of Postcolonial Fiction." In *Changing the Terms: Translating in the Postcolonial Era*, eds. Sherry Simon and Paul St. Pierre, 127–46. Ottawa: University of Ottawa Press.

Van den Abbeele, Georges. 1992. *Travel as Metaphor*. Minneapolis: University of Minnesota Press.

van Manen, Max. 1985. "Phenomenology of the Novel, or How Do Novels Teach?" *Phenomenology and Pedagogy* no. 3, 3: 177–87.

Williams, Raymond. 1976. *Keywords: A Vocabulary of Culture and Society*. London: Fontana.

Willinsky, John. 2001. *After Literacy*. New York: Peter Lang.

Wimsatt, W.K. Jr. and Munroe C. Beardsley. 1954. *The Verbal Icon: Studies in the Meaning of Poetry*. New York: Noonday Press/Farrar, Straus and Giroux.

Winterson, Jeanette. 1996. *Art Objects*. London, Ont.: Vintage.

———. 1989. *Sexing the Cherry*. London, Ont.: Vintage.

Witherell, Carol and Nel Noddings, eds. 1991. *Stories Lives Tell: Narrative and Dialogue in Education*. New York: Teachers College Press.

Wolff, Janice M. 1996. "Teaching in the Contact Zone: The Myth of Safe Houses." In *Critical Theory and the Teaching of Literature*, eds. J.F. Slevin and A. Young, 316–27. Urbana, Il: NCTE.

Wong, Jan. 1996. "The Olympians Were Welcomed Home, But Not Me." *The Globe and Mail*, August 10, D1.

Yep, Laurence. 1987. "A Chinese Sense of Reality." *Innocence and Experience: Essays and Conversations on Children's Literature*, eds. B. Harrison and G. Maguire. New York: Lothrop.

Young, Robert. 1990. *White Mythologies: Writing History and the West.* London: Routledge.

Index

—A—

Achebe, Chinua, 41, 70
achievement, educational, 15
aesthetics
    and canonicity, 45
    culture and, 28
    postcolonial pedagogy and, 144–47
Africa
    in British literature, 7–10
    migration to Britain from, 13
    in travel literature, 27
African Americans
    and American literature, 44–45, 64–69
    and literary canon, 20
    See also black literature
Alan (student), 105
Almon, Bert, 108
Altmann, Anna, 141
"Amaguduka at Glencoe Station" (Mtshali), 9
ambiguity, in interpretation, 80
Andrea (student), 102, 106, 144
"And Still I Rise" (Angelou), 100
Angelou, Maya, 100, 113
Anne (student), 106
Annie John (Kincaid), 113
"Another Part of the Sky" (Gordimer), 140
antiracist literature, 10, 128
apartheid, 8, 9, 10, 12, 98, 100–106
Apple, Michael, 78–79
Applebee, Arthur, 20–21, 24, 61, 81, 84, 125–26, 130, 141
Arnold, Matthew, 28, 43
Aronowitz, Stanley, 139
Ashcroft, Bill, 37, 38, 67
Asian Canadians, 74–76, 86, 88.
    See also Japanese Canadians
Asian literature, 74–76, 106–7
assimilationism
    in Britain, 16
    in Canada, 21
    in United States, 19
Atwood, Margaret, 22
Austen, Jane, 28

author, role of, in literary interpretation, 62

—B—

Bahri, Deepika, 35–36, 38–39
Bakhtin, Mikhail, 31–32, 33, 55, 83, 84, 111, 143
Baldwin, James, 20
Ballantyne, R. M., 9
Bannerji, Himani, 55
Barry, James, 106
Barthes, Roland, 54–55, 97, 104
Beardsley, Munroe C., 52
Becerra de Jenkins, Lyll, 100, 108
Bell, William, 108
Beloved (Morrison), 68, 116
Bhabha, Homi, 33, 36, 38, 97, 115
Biko, Steve, 98, 100, 105
bilingual education, 21
Birkerts, Sven, 83
Birney, Earle, 24
Bissoondath, Neil, 22
black literature, 17–19, 64–69
Blake, William, 43
Bloom, Alan, 43, 44
Bloom, Harold, 45–46
Bob (student), 118–19
Brad (student), 102
Brand, Dionne, 1, 27
Brenda (student), 119–20
Brian (student), 111
Brink, André, 70
Britain
    cultural identity of, 17
    literature curriculum in, 5
    multicultural education in, 14–19
    postcolonial pedagogy in, 65–66
    as postcolonial society, 17
Britzman, Deborah, 40, 64–65, 118, 121
Brown vs. *Board of Education of Topeka* (1954), 19
Bruner, Jerome, 28–29
Bruns, Gerald, 42
Buchan, John, 9
"B. Wordsworth" (Naipaul), 140

—C—

Calvinism, 8
Camera Lucida: Reflections on Photography (Barthes), 104
Cameron, Robert, 24, 61, 141
Canada
    immigration and, 41, 108, 136–37
    literature curriculum in, 1, 5, 23–24
    multicultural education in, 21–25
    national image of, 118–20
    postcolonial pedagogy in, 69–70
    racism in, 22, 118–20
    text selection in, 63
canon (literature)
    Anglo-American, 20–21
    boundaries of, 23
    British, 11–12
    Canadian, 1, 23–24
    criteria of, 42
    debates over, 5
    definition of, 42
    end of, 47
    expansion of, 111–12, 128, 131–32
    feminist critique of, 56
    formation of, 12, 42–47
    and mandatory texts, 17
    nomadic, 47
    pedagogical goals and, 24–25
    postcolonial literature and questioning of, 39
    universalism and, 16
Carlos (student), 92, 94
Catalan Atlas, 147–48
Cathy (student), 111
Césaire, Aimé, 33
Chambers, Iain, 30–31, 122, 125, 135, 136
Chang, Diana, 78
China, literature of, 75
Chinese Americans, and literary canon, 20
Chow, Wayne, 33
Choy, Wayson, 74
Chris (student), 87, 91
Christianity, 119–20
Christian National Education (South Africa), 9
Cisneros, Sandra, 100, 113
civil rights, in United States, 19–20
civil war, 107

Clay Marble, The (Minfong Ho), 100
Clifford, James, 29, 30
Coleridge, Samuel Taylor, 146
Colin (student), 105, 106, 141
Color Purple, The (Walker), 64
Commonwealth literature, 36–37
Congress of South African Writers, 10
conservatives
    and literary canon, 43, 45
    and multiculturalism in Britain, 15
    and multiculturalism in Canada, 21
contact-zone theory, 67–69
Convention on the Elimination of all Forms of Discrimination Against Women (1979), 14
Cooper, James Fenimore, 43
"Country Lovers" (Gordimer), 98, 100–106, 112, 140
Cox, Brian, 16
Cox Report, The, 16
critical pedagogy. *See* postcolonial pedagogy
critical thinking
    literature and, 1, 127
    postcolonial pedagogy as, 40
    See also literary interpretation
Cry Freedom (film), 98, 100, 101, 104–6, 112, 140
cultural literacy, 43
culture
    concept of, 28–29
    constructivist view of, 30
    dialogical approach to, 31–33
    differences in, 86, 87
    melting pot versus salad bowl concept of, 19
    politics and, 29–30
    See also identity: cultural
Culture and Anarchy (Arnold), 43
Culture and Imperialism (Said), 46–47
curriculum
    in Canada, 1
    change in, 18–19, 58–59, 113, 125, 132, 143
    goals of, and text selection, 24, 79
    multiculturalism in, 5, 12, 18–19
    quality as issue in, 19–20
    racism in, 18

representative cultural samplings in, 51–52
in South Africa, 7–12
and text selection, 63

—D—

Darbasie, Nigel, 108
Dark Child, The (Laye), 99–100
Dasenbrock, Reed Way, 61–63, 67
Dawn (student), 106
Deanna (student), 120, 138
deconstruction, 54, 62
Deleuze, Gilles, 6
Derrida, Jacques, 53, 54, 55
dialogical approach, to literary interpretation, 84–94, 129, 143
dialogue, 31–33, 84
Diamond, C. T. Patrick, 4
Diana (student), 143
Dias, Patrick, 23, 57–58, 80, 110
Dickens, Charles, 7, 8, 24, 43
Dimic, Milan, 23
Dirlik, Arif, 35
diversity, deficit versus difference approach to, 19
Donne, John, 7
Do the Right Thing (film), 70
Dry White Season, A (Brink), 70
Duncan, James, 27–28

—E—

Eaglestone, Robert, 24–25
Eagleton, Terry, 53–54
Eco, Umberto, 49–50
Eliot, T. S., 43
Elliot, Jean Leonard, 21
Empire Writes Back, The: Theory and Practice in Post-Colonial Literatures (Ashcroft, Griffiths, and Tiffin), 37
empowerment, multicultural education as, 21
Endless Steppe, The, 111
English as a Second Language, in Britain, 15
English for Ages 5 to 16, 16
"Equal Opportunity" (Wong-Chu), 108, 142

essentialism, 30–31, 33
ethnicity
essentialism and, 30–31
and student response to literature, 127–28, 137–39
ethnic minorities. *See* minorities
ethnography, 27
Eurocentrism, 8, 20, 46, 54, 84
European Convention of Human Rights (1950), 14
exam preparation, 24

—F—

Fanny (student), 109
Fanon, Franz, 33, 36
Farah (student), 110, 141
feminism
critique of poststructuralism and post-colonialism in, 55
curriculum critique by, 55–56
race and, 56
Ferré, Rosario, 78, 84, 93, 94, 138, 143
fiction. *See* literature
Fleras, Augie, 21
Forbidden City (Bell), 108, 111
Forster, E. M., 70
Foucault, Michel, 55
Fugitive Pieces (Michaels), 147–48

—G—

Galloway, Priscilla, 24
García Márquez, Gabriel, 33, 78
"A Very Old Man with Enormous Wings," 84, 91, 92, 137, 139
Garner, Hugh, 24
Gilbert, Pam, 56
Giroux, Henry, 44, 116, 139
Goebel, Bruce, 126
Goldberg, David, 29–30
Goldsmith, Oliver, 43
Goody, Joan, 15
Gorak, Jan, 47
Gordimer, Nadine, 10, 78, 116
"Another Part of the Sky," 140
"Country Lovers," 98, 100–106, 112, 140

"Happy Event," 84, 89, 90, 137, 139, 145
Graff, Gerald, 39, 79, 99, 111
Gray, Thomas, 43
great books. *See* canon (literature)
Great Britain. *See* Britain
Greene, Maxine, 77–78, 104, 132–33
Green Hills of Africa (Hemingway), 70
Greenlaw, James, 39–40, 69–70
Griffin, Joseph, 106
Griffiths, Gareth, 37, 67
Guattari, Felix, 6
Guillén, Claudio, 31
Gunn Allen, Paula, 146

—H—

Haggard, Henry Rider, 9
Hall, Catherine, 17, 115, 116
Hall, James C., 13, 79, 126
Hall, Stuart, 121–22
Hamilton, Virginia, 66
Hand Full of Stars, A (Schami), 99
Hansson, Gunnar, 58–59
"Happy Event" (Gordimer), 84, 89, 90, 137, 139, 145
Hardy, Thomas, 7, 8
Haroun and the Sea of Stories (Rushdie), 50
Harriet's Daughter (Nourbese Philip), 99
Hawthorne, Nathaniel, 43, 66
Hemingway, Ernest, 70
"Heritage Day" (Almon), 108
heritage languages, 21
Herrnstein-Smith, Barbara, 12
Hirsch, E. D., 43, 44
history, concept of, 4
Honorable Prison, The (Becerra de Jenkins), 100, 108, 111
hooks, bell, 7, 56, 61, 115
House of Dies Drear, The (Hamilton), 66
House on Mango Street, The (Cisneros), 100, 113
Huckleberry Finn (Twain), 64
human rights, and educational policy, 14
Hutcheon, Linda, 54
hybrid identities, 78, 136

—I—

identity
    construction of, 116, 123
    cultural, 17, 19, 33, 116–23
    hybrid, 78, 136
    imperialism and subaltern, 32
    language and, 31–32
    narrative and formation of, 132
    power and formation of, 33
    racial, 5, 29–30
I Know Why the Caged Bird Sings (Angelou), 113
imagination, reading and, 49, 50–51
immigrants and immigration
    to Britain, 15
    Canada and, 41, 108, 136–37
    educational experience of, 17–18
    and multicultural education, 13
    Western culture as product of, 41
"Immigrants: The Second Generation" (Irie), 108
imperialism
    and narrative, 46–47
    and postcolonialism, 36
    subaltern identity created by, 32
India, 13
International Covenant on Civil and Political Rights (1966), 14
International Day for the Elimination of Racism and Racial Discrimination, 100
international students. *See* minorities: students
Internet, 69–70
interpretation. *See* literary interpretation
intertextuality, 111
interviews with students, 104–6
Irie, Kevin, 108
Iser, Wolfgang, 56–57, 80
Itsuka (Kogawa), 122, 138

—J—

"Jade Peony, The" (Choy), 74
James, Henry, 43
Janet (student), 93
Janks, Hilary, 8
Japan, 69–70
Japanese Canadians, 117–22

Jared (student), 109, 110, 141
Jasmine (Mukherjee), 70
Jeff (student), 102–3, 112, 141
Jenny (student), 107
Jen (student), 87, 91
Joe (student), 105
Johnston, Ingrid, 141
John (student, grade 10), 103
John (student, grade 12), 93
Jon (student), 107
journey
    as metaphor for narrative, 135–36
    as metaphor for research, 2–3
Joy Luck Club, The (Tan), 138, 139
"Judge's Son, The" (Nicole), 140
June (student), 109
justice. *See* social justice
Justin (student), 105

—K—

"Kaffir, The" (Pringle), 9
Karen (student), 86, 89, 90, 93, 138, 145
Kien (student), 88, 90, 91, 92, 138
Kincaid, Jamaica, 35, 113
Kingman Report, The, 16
Kitchen God's Wife, The (Tan), 138
Knight, Hugh, 15
Kogawa, Joy, 27, 117–23, 138, 140
Kroetsch, Robert, 22
Krupat, Arnold, 30–31
Kwan (student), 88

—L—

Langer, Judith, 81, 84
language
    in Canadian education, 21
    and culture, 31–32
    and identity construction, 123
    student experience with, 88
Lanier, Douglas, 51
Laura (student), 94
Laurence, Margaret, 24, 78, 83, 85
Lawrence, D. H., 43
Laye, Camara, 100
Leavis, F. R., 43
Lee, Harper, 24, 99, 108, 140
Lee, Spike, 70

Leggo, Carl, 78, 83, 85
Ley, David, 27–28
literacy, 68
Literary Experiences Volume Two, 78
literary interpretation
    aesthetic versus political considera-
    tions in, 144–47
    context of work and, 52–53
    criteria of, 62
    dialogical approach to, 84–94, 129,
    143
    feminism and, 55–56
    poststructuralism and, 54–55
    reader-response criticism and, 56–57
    teacher role in, 62–63, 80, 129, 142–
    43
    See also critical thinking; student re-
    sponse to literature
literary theories
    feminism, 55–56
    New Criticism, 52–53, 144
    poststructuralism, 4, 53–55, 62, 80
    reader-response criticism, 56–58, 62,
    80
    structuralism, 53
    tacit, 51
literature
autobiography and, 11
    black, 17–19
    Commonwealth, 36–37
    minority, 20, 23
    Third World, 37
    See also antiracist literature; postcolo-
    nial literary studies; resistance lit-
    erature
Lorde, Audre, 13
"Love Must Not Be Forgotten" (Zhang Jie),
    106, 128
Lynch, James, 13–14
Lynn (student), 109

—M—

M*A*S*H* (television show), 107, 143
Mackey, Margaret, 49, 141
Malcolm X, 105
"Management of Grief, The" (Mukherjee),
    70
Mandela, Nelson, 100

Manivat, Vilas, 107–8
Many-Mouthed Birds: Contemporary Writing by Chinese Canadians (Lee and Wong-Chu), 75, 113
maps
    concept of, 6
    construction of, 147–48
Marlene (student), 141
Mary (student), 105, 106
McCarthy, Cameron, 43
McLaren, Peter, 64
McLeod, John, 37
Meg (high school English teacher), 73–146
    classroom preparation of, 141–42
    as English department head, 113, 144
    grade 10 class of, 97–113, 127, 128
    grade 11 AP class of, 115–23, 127, 128
    grade 12 class of, 84–95, 127
    and pedagogical change, 78–79
    and postcolonial pedagogy, 5–6, 81, 95, 111–12, 126–32
    student population taught by, 73–74, 98
    teaching background of, 73–74
    and text selection, 75–76, 79–80, 83, 98–100, 111–12, 113
Melinda (student), 87, 90
melting pot, culture as, 19
Melville, Herman, 43
Mhlope, Gcina, 145–46
Michaels, Anne, 147–48
Michael (student), 91
migrancy, as metaphor for identity, 136–37
Mike (student), 105, 109
Milton, John, 28, 43
Minfong Ho, 100
Minh-ha, Trinh, 11, 41–42, 73
minorities
    dispersal policy in Britain toward, 15
    students, 127, 129–30, 137–39, 143
minority literature, 20, 23
Mishima, Yukio, 106–7
Mistry, Rohinton, 23, 61
Mori, Kyoko, 147
Morrison, Toni, 19–20, 33, 44–45, 46, 105
    Beloved, 68, 116
"Mother Tongue" (Tan), 83, 88, 138
Mtshali, Oswald Mbuyiseni, 9

Mukherjee, Arun, 35, 108, 144–45
Mukherjee, Bharati, 70
multicultural education
    in Britain, 14–19
    in Canada, 21–25
    concept of, 13–14
    critical pedagogy in, 64–65
    cultural pluralism versus nationalism in, 21
    human rights and, 14
    immigration and, 13
    postcolonial literary studies and, 38–39
    principles for successful, 14
    in United States, 19–21
    See also postcolonial pedagogy
Multicultural Experiences (Applebee and Langer), 78, 81, 84
Multiculturalism, 108
multiculturalism
    as educational policy, 5
    liberal concept of, 115
multicultural textbooks, 15
Munro, Alice, 24
Myka (student), 121, 122–23, 138, 144
My Name is Seepeetza (Sterling), 100

—N—

Naidoo, Beverley, 65–66
Naipaul, V. S., 116, 140
narrative
    expansion of limits through, 11
    and identity formation, 132
    and imagination, 50–51
    and meaning, 4
    postmodern, 135
    as research tool, 3–4
National Curriculum (Britain), 17
Native Canadians, 69, 70, 85, 89, 113
Native Son (Wright), 64
Ndebele, Njabulo, 10
New Centenary Book of South African Verse, The (Slater), 8–9
New Criticism, 52–53, 144
Nicol, Abioseh, 116, 140
Nina (student), 85, 89, 137
No Longer at Ease (Achebe), 70

"Non-revolutionaries, The" (Yu-Wol
  Chong-Nyon), 107, 111
Nourbese Philip, Marlene, 22, 99
Nowlan, Alden, 24

—O—

Obasan (Kogawa), 117–23, 138
Okai, Atukwei, 116
Ondaatje, Michael, 116
orality, 68, 146
Orientalism (Said), 46
Orwell, George, 24
"Our Subdivision" (Darbasie), 108

—P—

Palumbo-Liu, David, 147
Passage to India, A (Forster), 70
Paton, Jonathan, 8
pedagogy. *See* postcolonial pedagogy
Peter (student), 94
photo/graphs
  concept of, 97–98
  of grade 10 class, 97–113
politics
  and culture, 29–30
  pedagogy and, 8
  and postcolonial literary studies, 67,
    147
Pope, Alexander, 43
postcolonialism
  concept of, 35–40
  and identity, 33
postcolonial literary studies
  authenticity in, 5
  concept of, 36–37
  mainstream students' benefits from,
    139
  minorities' benefits from, 137–39
  versus modernist tradition, 108
  multicultural education and, 38–39
  and politics, 67, 147
  postmodernism and, 54
  poststructuralism and, 54
  questions in, 63
  text selection for, 63, 75–80, 83, 98–
    100, 111–12, 113, 130–31, 141,
    149–53

postcolonial pedagogy
  aesthetics as issue in, 144–47
  and critical reading, 39–40, 51
  effect on student attitudes of, 132–33
  and identity construction, 123
  issues in, 2, 5–6, 84, 126, 144–45
  politics of teaching and, 64
  role of teaching strategy in, 80–81, 95,
    113
  and student response to literature, 58,
    121–22, 137–41, 144
  success and failure of, 112–13
  teacher-to-teacher transmission of, 129
  teacher workload for, 141–42
  teaching strategy for, 67–69
  See also multicultural education
postcolonial studies, 38.
  See also postcolonial literary studies
postmodernism, 54, 135–36
poststructuralism
  and ambiguity, 80
  and literary interpretation, 53–55
  principles of, 4
  See also deconstruction
power
  and canon formation, 42, 44, 46
  in ethnography, 27–28
  identity formation and, 33
  in literary education, 28
Pratt, Mary Louise, 67, 125
Prester John (Buchan), 9
Pringle, Thomas, 9

—Q—

Quayson, Ato, 73

—R—

race
  as cultural category, 29–30
  essentialism and, 30–31
  and feminism, 56
  and identity, 5
racism
  in Canada, 22, 118–20
  in curriculum, 18
  as curriculum topic, 98–99, 100, 108,
    112, 139–40

and educational achievement, 15
in European literature, 10
postcolonial pedagogy and analysis of, 40
student experiences of, 85, 89, 91, 106, 120, 121–22
student responses to, 102, 103, 104, 110, 118–19
as subject of literature, 64–69
See also apartheid
Rau, Santha Rama, 78, 83, 85
reader-response criticism, 56–58, 62, 80
reading, experience of, 49–50. *See also* literary interpretation
realism, 52–53
reception theory. *See* reader-response criticism
research
    journey as metaphor for, 2–3
    narrative used in, 3–4
    as photo/graph, 97–98, 104
    qualitative, 3
    See also interviews with students
resistance literature, 10
"Return to India" (Rau), 85
Road to Memphis, The (Taylor), 99, 100, 108, 110–11
Rob (student), 86
Roll of Thunder, Hear My Cry (Taylor), 65–66, 99
Rosenblatt, Louise, 57
Rushdie, Salman, 33, 36–37, 50, 97, 136
Ryan, Simon, 41
Ryle, Martin, 146

—S—

Said, Edward, 46–47, 146
salad bowl, culture as, 19
Sally (student), 105
Samantrai, Ranu, 23
Saussure, Ferdinand de, 53
Scafe, Suzanne, 17–19
Scarlet Letter, The (Hawthorne), 66
Schami, Rafik, 99
Scott, Walter, 43
Selling Illusions: The Cult of Multiculturalism in Canada (Bissoondath), 22
Senghor, Leopold, 33

Sepamla, Sipho, 10–11
sexism, in Canadian canon, 24
Shabanu, Daughter of the Wind (Staples), 108
Shakespeare, William, 7, 8, 24, 43
Shane (student), 92
Sharleen (student), 104, 105
Shaw, George Bernard, 7
Simon (student), 85
slave narratives, 66
Slemon, Stephen, 38
Smagorinsky, Peter, 63–64
small group reading, 109–11, 129–30, 143
social justice, 90, 119–20
Sofia (student), 86, 89, 91, 94
Souster, Raymond, 24
South Africa, 4
    as curriculum topic, 98, 100–101
    literature curriculum in, 7–12
Spears-Bunton, Linda, 66–67
Spivak, Gayatri, 32
"Spring Storm" (Yoko), 69–70
standardized testing, in Britain, 17
Staples, Suzanne Fisher, 108
Steinbeck, John, 24
Steiner, Wendy, 50, 51
Sterling, Shirley, 100
stories. *See* narrative
Storyteller, The: Short Stories from Around the World (Barry and Griffin), 106
structuralism, 53
student experience
    backgrounds and, 73–74, 98
    broadening through literature of, 11, 16, 92, 122–23, 139, 147
    classroom instruction and, 15
    as deterrent to reading, 74–76, 121–22
    immigrants', 17–18, 127
    and literary interpretation, 57–58
    literature curriculum and, 1
    of racism, 85, 89, 91, 106, 120, 121–22
student response to literature
    accessibility of postcolonial literature, 84
    and attitude change, 132–33
    class context and, 107, 123, 129
    dialogical approach, 84–94, 129, 143
    ethnicity and, 127–28, 137–39

resistance to multicultural literature, 64–66, 74–76, 112–13, 117–18, 127–28
in small groups, 110, 129–30
unpopular sentiments, 121–22
subalterns, 32
Su-Lin (student), 94
Sumara, Dennis, 52
Survival (Atwood), 22
Susan (English teacher), 125
Susan (student), 102
"Swaddling Clothes" (Mishima), 106–7, 130
Swann Report, The, 15–16

—T—

Tammy (student), 102
Tan, Amy, 33, 78
"Mother Tongue," 83, 88, 138
"Two Kinds," 83, 86, 87, 138, 139
"Tangled" (Leggo), 85
Taylor, Charles, 6
Taylor, Mildred
The Road to Memphis, 99, 100, 108, 110–11
Roll of Thunder, Hear My Cry, 65–66, 99
teacher education
multicultural education and reform in, 14
support for postcolonial pedagogy in, 131
teachers
demands on, 125–26, 143
and noncanonical texts, 61–63, 65, 141
role of, in literary interpretation, 62–63, 80, 129, 142–43
support systems for, 131, 141–42
textbooks, multicultural, 15, 131
text selection
in Canada, 63
for classes by grade, 149–53
community reaction to, 130
curriculum goals and, 24, 79
for Meg's grade 10 class, 98–100, 111–12, 113
for Meg's grade 12 class, 75–80, 83

process of, 141–42
support for teachers in, 131
See also canon (literature)
theories. *See* literary theories
Third Space, 115
Third World literature, 37
Thomson, Jack, 49, 55
Tiffin, Helen, 37, 67
"Toilet, The" (Mhlope), 145–46
To Kill a Mockingbird (Lee), 99, 108, 110–11, 112, 140–41
tolerance, as outcome of multicultural education, 21–22, 40
Tompkins, Jane, 57, 95
translation, and accessibility of text, 106, 107, 112, 128, 145
travel
and identity formation, 41–42, 123
as metaphor for teaching literature, 51–52
and representation, 27–28
Tredell, Nicolas, 55
Twain, Mark, 43, 64
"Two Kinds" (Tan), 83, 86, 87, 138, 139
Tymoczko, Maria, 139

—U—

UNESCO Declaration on Race and Racial Prejudice (1978), 14
United Nations Declaration of Human Rights (1948), 14
United States
literature curriculum in, 5, 19–21
multicultural education in, 19–21
postcolonial pedagogy in, 66–69

—V—

Van den Abbeele, Georges, 1, 2
van Manen, Max, 50
Verbal Icon, The (Wimsatt and Beardsley), 52
"Very Old Man with Enormous Wings, A" (García Márquez), 84, 91, 92, 137–38, 139

—W—

Walker, Alice, 64

Weiner, Gerry, 100, 112, 140
Western culture
    concept of, 44
    immigration and production of, 41
West Indies, 13, 15
"Where the World Began" (Laurence), 83, 85
"Who Needs It?" (Manivat), 107–8
Williams, Raymond, 28
Willinsky, John, 49
Wimsatt, W. K., 52
Winterson, Jeanette, 7, 135
Wolff, Janice M., 67–69
Wong, Jan, 136–37
Wong-Chu, Jim, 108, 142
Woods, Donald, 98, 100, 105
Wordsworth, William, 7, 8, 28
Wright, Richard, 64

—Y—

Yep, Lawrence, 20
Yoko, Mori, 69–70
Young, Robert, 54
"Youngest Doll, The" (Ferré), 84, 93, 94, 138, 139, 143
"Youth Our Best Hope to End Racial Discrimination" (Weiner), 100, 140
Yu-Wol Chong-Nyon, 107

—Z—

Zhang Jie, 106

ABOUT THE AUTHOR

 INGRID JOHNSTON is Associate Professor in the Department of Secondary Education at the University of Alberta, Canada. She received her B.A. and University Education Diploma from the University of Natal, South Africa, and her M.Ed. and Ph.D. from the University of Alberta. She teaches courses and conducts research in English education, curriculum studies, postcolonial theories, and issues of culture and teacher education. She has published widely in international journals and has written several book chapters related to postcolonial and multicultural literary studies.

Studies in the Postmodern Theory of Education

General Editors
Joe L. Kincheloe & Shirley R. Steinberg

Counterpoints publishes the most compelling and imaginative books being written in education today. Grounded on the theoretical advances in criticalism, feminism, and postmodernism in the last two decades of the twentieth century, Counterpoints engages the meaning of these innovations in various forms of educational expression. Committed to the proposition that theoretical literature should be accessible to a variety of audiences, the series insists that its authors avoid esoteric and jargonistic languages that transform educational scholarship into an elite discourse for the initiated. Scholarly work matters only to the degree it affects consciousness and practice at multiple sites. Counterpoints' editorial policy is based on these principles and the ability of scholars to break new ground, to open new conversations, to go where educators have never gone before.

For additional information about this series or for the submission of manuscripts, please contact:

> Joe L. Kincheloe & Shirley R. Steinberg
> c/o Peter Lang Publishing, Inc.
> 275 Seventh Avenue, 28th floor
> New York, New York 10001

To order other books in this series, please contact our Customer Service Department:

> (800) 770-LANG (within the U.S.)
> (212) 647-7706 (outside the U.S.)
> (212) 647-7707 FAX

Or browse online by series:

> www.peterlangusa.com